ID0649608

BE A MAN

BE A MAN

THE ULTIMATE GUIDE

THE BE A MAN GUY

AS TOLD BY
JOE McCALL

WITH
MISHKA SHUBALY

HARPER PERENNIAL

NEW YORK • LONDON • TORONTO • SYDNEY • NEW DELHI • AUCKLAND

HARPER ● PERENNIAL

HarperCollins books may be purchased for educational, business, or sales promotional use. For information, please email the Special Markets Department at SPsales@harpercollins.com.

FIRST EDITION

Designed by Jen Overstreet

Library of Congress Cataloging-in-Publication Data has been applied for.

ISBN 978-0-06-327267-5

22 23 24 25 26 LSC 10 9 8 7 6 5 4 3 2 1

CONTENTS

INTRODUCTION

HERE WE ARE

I've been busting my ass for the past fifty years. I've seen every scam, I've run every hustle, from running numbers for bookies to every kind of construction to private security to processing mortgages and buying real estate. A few years back, I started to think about settling down and retiring, sitting by the pool with a scotch on the rocks and just watching the clock run out. Then *Be a Man* exploded across social media and completely changed the course of my life. Now in the twilight of my career, I have been thrust into the role of the Godfather of the Be a Man Mafia.

We call it the Be a Man Mafia because even if I wanted to get out, the Mafia wouldn't let me. These days, I can barely walk down the street without some maniac yelling, "Be a Man," out of the window of a passing car or someone pulling over to the side of the road to ask for a picture to show their friends. For years, I lived happily in the shadows. Now complete strangers are walking up and asking me for advice on how to "Be a Man" when I'm taking a piss. So instead of doing a stop and chat with every asshole for the next twenty years, I wrote a book to serve as the Ultimate Guide. Now leave me alone.

BE A MAN

The Struggle Isn't Real, It's Everything

Work harder, not smarter. **Be a Man.**

These days, every young guy is looking for the easy way out. They want to cut corners at work, they want to get rich quick, they want to pick up girls with no effort. Since I was a little boy, I was always taught never to take shortcuts, that the road to success was a back-breaking one. We grew up framing houses by hand for shit pay, we worked long days at multiple jobs and somehow only made enough money to still be broke, we put in countless hours buying way too many drinks at smoke-filled local dives trying to pick up women.

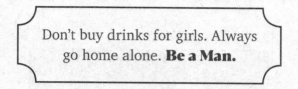

Don't buy drinks for girls. Always go home alone. **Be a Man.**

There were no YouTube tutorials, no cryptocurrencies that could make you a millionaire overnight, no dating apps you could use to handpick Filipino chicks under five feet tall who like dogs and Jack Daniel's. We were taught to work for everything . . . and that's the way we liked it. If you really want to be a man, here's a helpful life hack: life hacks are for cowards. The hardest way is the only way.

Don't take the elevator. Take the stairs. **Be a Man.**

As men, we've always been on a mission to do it our way, no matter how difficult or ridiculous it might seem to everyone else. As far back as I can remember, my brothers and I learned life lessons by doing chores around the house. My dad didn't wait for the perfect conditions or supply us with the best tools for the job, he *made* us struggle in order to learn. This is a lesson I have applied in all facets of life over the past five decades. It's not just about taking the scenic route instead of taking a shortcut, it's about abandoning all possible routes in favor of the longest, most nerve-shredding, life-threatening, inches-wide coyote path on the side of an unforgiving cliff till you feel like you're losing your fucking mind from terror and regret.

> Don't let anyone ruin your day.
> Ruin it yourself. **Be a Man.**

When the leaves fall off the trees in November here in New England, the northeast wind blows and they go everywhere. Cleaning them up can quickly turn into a month-long project. Just when you think you're done, a strong gust of wind out of nowhere blows everything from your lazy prick next-door neighbor's yard into yours and you're back to square one.

I've been told that leaves rake best when they're light and crisp, but I wouldn't know. While the eager beavers were out there as soon as the first leaves dropped, we grew up with a different, more challenging approach. We would ALWAYS get our leaf assignments fresh off of a nor'easter. Those light, crisp leaves would soak up water until they weighed as much as wet concrete and smelled like the flooded basement of an abandoned insane asylum. My dad said it was good that the leaves were heavy because it made for a better workout. "You don't have to go to the gym today. Lucky you."

> Blow your leaves onto your
> neighbor's lawn. **Be a Man.**

When we had to paint the house, there were no sprayers, no rollers, no fancy blue tape for the windows. There was a brush, a bucket, and a "don't fuck anything up" pep talk. Any asshole can use a roller on a wall but painting the edges next to windows with a brush taught us how to do the job right. No one ever became great at anything by putting in the least amount of effort. Sometimes in life, struggle and hardship are exactly what we need.

> Don't take the easy way out. Struggle at all costs. **Be a Man.**

A STRUGGLE FOR EVERY SEASON

FALL is all about harvesting and cashing in on the hard work you put in all year long. Time to hunt, gather, and prepare for the winter. Spend a thousand dollars at Costco on canned chili and booze in plastic jugs.

Don't use a log splitter. Chop three cords of hickory by hand. Be a Man.

WINTER has always been synonymous with things like death, pain, and being miserable. It has always been a time to reset, throw on twenty pounds, and hibernate. We only leave the house for the essentials and when we do, we are wearing shorts.

> Don't use a snowblower. Shovel the whole driveway by hand. Be a Man.

SPRING is when everything and everyone comes to life. The birds return, the flowers are blooming, and the squirrels and other vermin emerge from hibernation. This is the perfect time to start tackling those jobs in the yard and on the exterior of the house that you have been contemplating all winter while the girls shed their North Face jackets.

> Don't use a nail gun. Hammer till your fucking arm falls out of the socket. Be a Man.

SUMMER is the only time we really feel alive. On a hot summer day with the top down on the car, we feel like we are twenty years old again. The world is full of possibilities and we feel like we can do anything: get a bad case of poison ivy, get a case of the clap, get a DUI.

> Take all the groceries in one trip, in one hand, and cut all your circulation off. Be a Man.

Born to Be a Man

Every day after school from when I was nine years old, I hung out in my uncle's bar, the American House Café, down the street from my house in East Boston. I can still smell the beer and the booze-soaked hardwood floors and the smoke from a dozen lit Marlboros wafting through the air.

Rip butts till you're dead. **Be a Man.**

Most days consisted of me sitting on the bar drinking Cokes from the fountain as the neighborhood drunks, shipyard workers, and degenerate gamblers stumbled through the door. Some were there for a drink but most of them were there to place a bet with my Uncle Libby. Other kids learned how to do math in school, but I learned by sticking close to my uncle. Libby drove big red Cadillacs, and always wore a suit and glasses with a pen behind his ear and a folded-up newspaper under his arm. His hair smelled like Tres Flores pomade and he liked to keep a glass of water on top of the fridge because he said it kept it cold. He was married once for nine months but his wife chased him through Day Square in East Boston with an axe one afternoon. Libby always had a wad of cash on him as thick as a two-by-four. If you wanted to gamble on the horses or the Celtics back in those days, there was no credit: you had to show up with the cash plus the vig in hand to get in on the action.

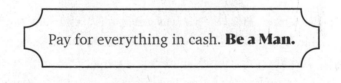

Pay for everything in cash. **Be a Man.**

Libby's brother, my Uncle Nacco, worked the front of the house, serving drinks and running the day-to-day while Libby ran the books. Italians were a different breed back then. These two brothers ran a business together, they sat ten feet apart all day long, but they still barely spoke to each other. They liked to use me as a carrier pigeon, walking back and forth across the room to relay messages, even though they could both hear what the other was saying. I could see them perk up the minute I walked into the room and over to the bar.

"Your uncle is being a real prick today, you know," Nacco muttered as he handed me a wad of cash.

When I walked over to hand it to Libby, he snapped back, "Tell Nacco to go fuck himself!"

The only time I ever heard one of them say something nice about the other was the day we got raided. Two cops busted through the side door. Libby tucked his newspaper under his arm, put his hat on real low, and made his way to the back door. Before he could slip out, a cop grabbed him by the arm and slammed him against the wall.

Nacco stood up and yelled, "Get your fucking hands off him, he's an old man."

> Always talk shit about your family, but if someone else does it, fight 'em. **Be a Man.**

The American House Café was never busy, and that's the way they liked it. They served a couple of kinds of beer, whiskey, scotch, pretzels, and the occasional sandwich or burger. Nothing crazy. Most bars rely on booze to keep the doors open, but not here. Guys rolling their paychecks on a thoroughbred in the last race at Belmont is what moved the needle.

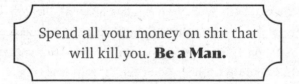

> Spend all your money on shit that will kill you. **Be a Man.**

Most people would say the inside of a seedy bar is no place for a kid but I learned more inside those four walls than I ever learned in school. One day, one of the regular delivery guys walked through the empty barroom and grabbed a fistful of dollars out of the tip jar on his way out the door. I was tucked away in the corner and saw the whole thing but he never saw me. As soon as he got around the corner, I ran into the kitchen and told my uncles what happened. They nearly ran me over as they flew out of the bar and grabbed the delivery guy before he was able to drive off. They got every dime back and gave the driver a few lumps as a parting gift. When they got back inside, they sat me down to tell me they were proud of me for letting them know. They also made it clear that being a snitch was no way to live. Unless, of course, you were protecting your family.

FIVE RITES OF PASSAGE: BECOMING A MAN

1. **CAUGHT SMOKING.** When you get caught with a cigarette and your old man makes you smoke the whole pack, finish it. Then ask him to buy you another one.

2. **WORKING ON YOUR BIKE.** When you don't really know what you're doing but want to feel like a man, constantly flip your bike upside down and grease the chain.

3. **CRACKING THE LIQUOR CABINET.** Breaking into the coveted liquor cabinet and stealing some sort of booze to get drunk is part of growing

up. But when you are this young, you don't really know your way around. Chug a bottle of margarita mix and wonder why you don't get wasted.

4. **ADULT ENTERTAINMENT.** Every guy has stashed porno mags in a bag in the closet, in the shed, or in a ditch in the woods. When you hide these under your bed, your mom will immediately find them. Act dumbfounded and deny that they are yours.

5. **SHOPLIFTING.** Some people can do this in their sleep while others are terrified to swipe a stick of gum. If you shoplift, make sure it's something you don't want and you can't use.

Let It Ride

The year 1966 was the year everything changed for me. On June 8, the American Football League and National Football League announced their merger, catapulting football to the forefront of American sports.

> Don't go to church on Sunday. Sit on the couch and watch football for eight hours. **Be a Man.**

That fall, I was a third-grader moonlighting as a bookie in training. While most eight-year-olds were collecting sports cards and watching the game on TV, I was watching their fathers and uncles lose money on Sunday and pay my uncles the next day. Every Monday, my Uncle Libby would pick me up after school in his big boat Cadillac DeVille. "Get in the car kid, we're going to Southie to collect." I swear to God, that car was a mile long.

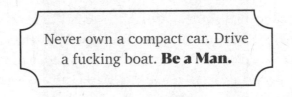

Never own a compact car. Drive a fucking boat. **Be a Man.**

I wasn't just seeing the game from the sidelines. Before long, I was also getting in on the action. My dad would bring home football pick 'em cards from the post office. It was a one-dollar entry and if you picked four games right, you could win ten bucks. By junior high, 1 was running my own cards. Within a month, I was raking in twenty dollars a week. Before too long, I got ratted out. It was a whole ordeal—I was called to the office and questioned by the police chief.

While some families are torn apart by the pitfalls of gambling, we built a bond over the thrills of victory and the agony of defeat. In the mid-1960s, Rockingham Park in New Hampshire was one of the country's premier racetracks. A Saturday in the summer would often see 15,000 people pouring through the gates. Some of my most memorable days growing up were when we headed to "the Rock" for the day to take in the races with Nacco. My uncle was such an avid gambler that he knew everyone at the track by name. We would show up so early they wouldn't even be open yet. We'd walk around the side of the building and at 9:00 A.M. on the nose, the side door swung open and we'd scurry in.

> Always be early, then get mad when people aren't there yet. **Be a Man.**

A short bald guy with a limp and big cigar hanging out of his mouth led us down a dark hallway and into the kitchen area. Before we knew it, we were sitting down, eating eggs and flapjacks with the jockeys and the trainers. As a kid this seemed totally normal but when we got older, we found out there was nothing normal about getting to eat breakfast with the jockeys before a race.

> Always know a guy who knows a guy. **Be a Man.**

One hot summer afternoon, we were all standing down by the fence watching the jockeys parade their horses before the race. My little brother Joe was standing on the fence when he looked over his shoulder at me.

"Hey, Harmon, the number five horse is ninety-nine to one."

I looked up at the board.

"You got a good feeling about that one, huh?"

Ninety-nine to one is the worst possible odds that can be posted on the tote board. The tote board literally couldn't go any higher. The horse was probably some worn out bag of bones that would be dog food by the end of the week. Still, throwing a buck on a long shot isn't the worst idea. You can make a bundle if the horse wins.

Throw all your money on a long shot. **Be a Man.**

I walked around the patio and shot the shit with the guys as I kept my eyes on the board to see where the money was going. The number five horse started getting money thrown on it. The action was hot all the way up to race time, with the number five horse closing at twenty-five to one. So still an outsider, but nowhere near the long shot it had been. Did someone know something we didn't? We'd soon find out.

It wasn't even that close. The number five horse pushed out early. By the time the race was over, number five won by four lengths. My little brother walked over to me and Nacco with his head down.

"What's up, Joe?" my uncle sputtered.

"I think I messed up," he said, looking down at his feet.

"What the fuck are you talking about?" Nacco said.

"I think the jockey on the number five horse was signaling the guy next to me, he was looking right at him and tapping his leg."

Back in those days, there were always people trying to fix and manipulate the outcome, anyone that had inside information might use the tip of the cap or a tap on the leg to signal that a fix was in.

Nacco threw down his program and started pacing around.

"Why didn't you say anything?"

"I wasn't sure," Joe mumbled.

Nacco was furious.

"What, did you want the horse to come over and tell you himself?"

Joe shrugged without looking up.

"I would have thrown ten across the board, we would have been riding home in a limousine tonight," Nacco snarled.

The ride home that night was the longest hour of my life. My brother Joe had fucked up and my uncle never, ever let him forget it for as long as he lived.

> If someone makes a mistake, ride them relentlessly about it forever. **Be a Man.**

Once, when I was in high school, my dad hit for a big trifecta at Wonderland Dog Track. He called me and my buddies in for backup when he collected the money. (Walking out of that hellhole with seven Gs would put a target on your back for all the desperate guys who had lost the mortgage payment that day.) My pop was all about principles. When the cashier paid out my father's $7,531 but didn't immediately hand him his ten cents, Pop was ready to go through the glass and pull the cashier's shirt over his head. Did he really need the ten cents? Of course not. But it was the principle of it. He felt like someone was trying to get one over on him. That was something he would never let slide.

> Never trust anyone. They're all trying to rip you off. **Be a Man.**

FIVE BEST PIECES OF GAMBLING ADVICE

1. Bet on yourself. You can't trust anyone else anyway.

2. Only gamble what you're willing to lose.

3. Always bet the "under in day games" and the "over in primetime games." If the players party the night before it always takes them till late in the day to fully recover and perform.

4. Your rent money always gets the best returns.

5. Never gamble.

The Good Ole Days

In the late 1950s and early 1960s, men were cut from a different cloth. They went to work, they put food on the table, and they kept to themselves. They smoked butts, drank scotch, and showed absolutely no emotion. There was no hug from dad when he came home or a barrage of encouraging words. You respected him and stayed out of his fucking way. Back in those days, men were stoic and gruff. They didn't talk about their feelings, they stuck to their guns and held grudges forever. Tough love is the greatest love of all.

> Don't show your feelings. Suppress them, bottle 'em up. **Be a Man.**

My old man was the youngest of seven kids and worked for the United States Postal Service as a mailman in Boston for forty-two years. While his brothers took a different path, he was in the rat race like De Niro in *A Bronx Tale* (but with an angry streak like De Niro in *Raging Bull*). Every day, he trekked through the rain, the snow, or the blazing summer heat to put food on the table. He was a rugged, barrel-chested ox who wasn't afraid to say whatever wild, off-the-wall, batshit crazy thought crossed his mind. Although it wasn't always what people wanted to hear, he taught us that being honest was the best way to handle everything.

> If you say something stupid, instead of apologizing, double down. **Be a Man.**

Pop spoke his own language, a mixture of street sayings and Italian proverbs that he lived by. He called wimpy guys "gentle" and crazy guys "soft." If you were drunk, you were "feeling good." If you were hungover, you "had a big head." At dinner, he would ask you a hundred times if you were full. He never called anyone by their name, it was always "What's he doing over there?" and "How's your wife?" Half of the time, we didn't even know what the fuck he was talking about, but we grew to love the humor it produced. Pop was a tough bastard with a short temper and if you crossed him once, he was finished with you.

> Hold a grudge until you die. **Be a Man.**

My parents didn't get out very much. Growing up, we hung out around the house or in the neighborhood. Our go-to clubhouse was my parents' basement. The floors had those cracked asbestos green tiles, the walls were half-painted fake wood paneling, and the cast iron pipes hung so low that you were destined for a concussion. The smell of gasoline mixed with mildew and mold filled the room. That dark dungeon was a haven for manliness.

> Find the grossest part of your house and spend all your time there. **Be a Man.**

In our house, the men and the women never hung out together. When my parents' friends would come over on a Saturday night, the ladies would stay upstairs to drink coffee and talk about life, and the men would retreat to the basement to drink liquor and play dice.

> Drink whiskey and chase it with whiskey. **Be a Man.**

Playing dice was a religion for Italians. My pop had jobs for all of the kids to ensure the game ran smoothly. My two little brothers were part of the action. Joe made sandwiches for anyone who wanted one. Carlo was the retriever. Every time the dice rattled off the wall, Carlo would run over and scoop 'em up and run 'em back to me. It was my job to blow on the dice to keep them clean and collect all the money.

> Loan your friends money to gamble with, then take them for everything they own. **Be a Man.**

The games were always full of action. You could feel the energy mounting, coursing through the air till finally someone threw the dice off of someone else's head. Then a fight would break out and end the night. Everyone would leave pissed off, talking trash—"I'll never throw dice with that cheat again!" The next week, they would do it all over.

FIVE REASONS TO FIGHT YOUR FRIENDS

1. That guy is crazy.

2. That guy is making me crazy.

3. He always touches his face before he eats.

4. He looked at me funny.

5. He had it coming.

Anytime, Anywhere

When we're young, we have our whole lives in front of us. It feels like we're going to live forever. We tell ourselves that we're gonna spend a whole winter living in a van and skiing in Aspen, or a summer bartending on Martha's Vineyard. We're gonna start a band, we're gonna start a casino, we're gonna restore a '69 Camaro from the ground up, we're gonna hitchhike to Alaska and work on a fishing boat.

Live out of your car. **Be a Man.**

All of these ideas seem within reach and fully possible, ripe and juicy and ready for the taking. Then life starts to come at you. You get a girlfriend, you get a car payment, you get an apartment. Bills start to pile up, and you get a job to support your new liabilities. This new job is most likely one you can't stand but it's paying the bills so you keep on showing up. Then one morning you wake up, thirty years later, wondering what the fuck just happened.

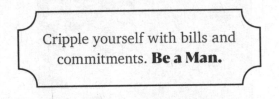

Cripple yourself with bills and commitments. **Be a Man.**

We take this path for several reasons: convenience, laziness, and fear of the unknown. We should be running in the opposite direction of this boring, bullshit dead-end grind, away from the comfort zones we create. We want to live and die like Vikings . . . but most times the manliest choice is to choose to do the shit that kills us slowly: nine-to-five jobs, late nights staring at the TV, Dunkin' Donuts, and Papa John's. But before you settle into a depressing, meager, and lonely existence, make sure to, at least once in your life, jump blindly into the deep end.

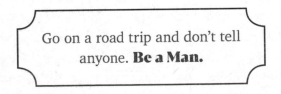

Go on a road trip and don't tell anyone. **Be a Man.**

When I was a kid, we made a point of throwing ourselves into uncomfortable situations. We would go on road trips at the drop of a hat. We'd go to Old Orchard Beach, Cape Cod, Atlantic City, Montreal, Fort Lauderdale, and Chicago. The main motivation that got us in a car to drive just about anywhere was usually hanging out with girls and partying. Looking back, most of the time the journey was far more enjoyable than the party ever was.

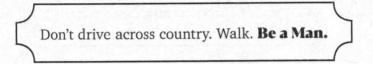

Don't drive across country. Walk. **Be a Man.**

There is something about the open road that makes us feel alive. Throwing some clothes in a trash bag, getting in a car, filling up the tank, and going places you've only heard about . . . there's nothing else like it. Going on an adventure with the boys requires little planning and always delivers a ton of fun. Although kamikaze road trips might not be the most responsible thing to do or make great financial sense, there are times you need to just burn the boats. When there's no safety net, you have experiences and learn things you never would otherwise.

Don't take swimming lessons. Jump in the deep end and sink like a rock. **Be a Man.**

Take Montreal. Strip clubs in America can be great in cities like Vegas and Atlanta but back in the day, Montreal strip clubs were legendary. In the '70s and '80s, there were over forty clubs in the city limits. These weren't hole-in-the-wall establishments either. Club Wanda's was five floors and 15,000 square feet. These were playgrounds for the boys to have fun and take in the sights.

Any time we headed to Canada, it was a different type of adventure. Those trips had layers to them. After a couple-hour drive, our first goal was to get the pot and drinks past the border patrol. Then we focused on getting to Montreal and hitting the strip clubs to get our shine on. Then we would find some French broads to drink with at the beer halls. Hanging out with girls that spoke another language always made for an interesting experience.

> Hit on a stripper or a cocktail waitress that you have absolutely no chance with. **Be a Man.**

One time, we were at the Old Munich in Montreal drinking all day. There was this tough old French broad sitting right next to us, going drink for drink. By five o'clock, we were pretty sauced up. Finally, this old broad falls right out of her chair. She had dropped dead right next to us, her glass in her hand. When the ambulance came, we helped load her up on the gurney. To honor her, we didn't move from our seats even after they took her out. We sat there and drank all night till they made us leave.

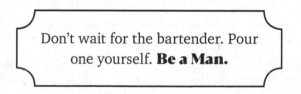

> Don't wait for the bartender. Pour one yourself. **Be a Man.**

When I was nineteen, I went on my first coast-to-coast, cross-country trip with some buddies. We planned to take I-90 across to Chicago, then the legendary Route 66 all the way down through

Illinois, Missouri, Oklahoma, Texas, New Mexico, and Arizona to Santa Monica.

Any time we went anywhere, we liked to drive until we couldn't drive anymore. It was a hot summer night at about 2:00 A.M. somewhere in central Michigan when we hit the wall. We saw an old beat-up billboard on the side of the road for a campground and took the next exit.

When we pulled in, there were no lights on in the office and everyone had turned in for the night in camping spots. We were goggle-eyed from driving but still looking to party so we pulled all the way to the back and set up our tents in a big field behind the campground. We were far enough away that us drinking and smoking and busting each other's balls didn't wake anyone. It must have been 4:00 A.M. before we finally passed out.

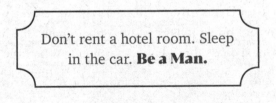

Don't rent a hotel room. Sleep in the car. **Be a Man.**

We got woken up in the morning by the owner of the grounds on a four-wheeler asking us, "What the fuck are you boys doing out here?" I told him we weren't trying to bother anyone because we came in so late. He said, "You some brave sonsabitches. You boys camped out right in the middle of one of the biggest rattlesnake fields in the country."

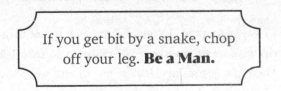

If you get bit by a snake, chop off your leg. **Be a Man.**

FIVE TIPS FOR TRAVELING LIKE A MAN

1. **LAST-MINUTE PACKING.** Women start putting together outfits and laying things out on the bed three weeks before the trip. Men put absolutely no thought into this process. If we are leaving the house at two o'clock, we start throwing shit in a contractor bag at one thirty.

2. **THE ESSENTIALS.** Don't overthink this process but there are some staples that you must have on any trip. While she is packing three outfits a day with a different pair of shoes for every outfit, we are going with the essentials: underwear, socks, a couple of T-shirts, one pair of pants, and a roll of quarters.

3. **THE CARRY-ON.** This is a trick I learned a long time ago. If it doesn't fit in the carry-on, it's not coming. Consolidate everything into the bag you take on the plane. This way you get in and out of the airport quickly and no one else can lose your shit besides you.

4. **GO SHOPPING WHEN THE PLANE LANDS.**
There are some things you don't take on purpose, like a toothbrush. This gives you an excuse to leave the hotel and run some errands alone to scope out your new surroundings.

5. **NEVER PLAN.** In a woman's perfect world, she wants a man who puts in the time and effort to map out the ultimate vacation. Men are the opposite—we like to plan everything except vacation. It doesn't matter how much your girl pesters you, don't think about any vacation stuff till you're there and it's happening in front of you. When she melts down, remind her of all the times she nagged you to be spontaneous. If she doesn't like that, maybe next year you'll get to go on vacation alone.

Stubborn as a Mule

In the summer of 1979, when I was twenty, I went on a camping trip with a bunch of college buddies. We had six cars in the convoy, loaded top to bottom with beers, fireworks, and red meat, bombing up I-93 North toward New Hampshire. I was driving my '69 Plymouth Fury with two of my boys, determined to get to the campground first and secure a prime location. About an hour into the trip, I declared to the boys that I was about to pull off the shortcut of all shortcuts, guaranteeing that this move would knock off at least a half hour from our time. Making good time is the ultimate man flex.

> Drive with the radio off unless
> someone tries to talk to you, then turn
> it all the way up. **Be a Man.**

I thought I knew what I was doing. I had driven these back-roads many times before. But this time they started to feel unfamiliar. The more lost I got, the more I stuck to my guns that this was all part of my plans. As we neared the Canadian border, I realized that I'd been driving so long that both of my friends had passed out. I quietly turned around and headed back to take the more familiar way. By the time I finally pulled into the campground, the sun was starting to rise over the mountains. Fuck it, I left my buddies to sleep in the car and never had to admit to wrongdoing.

> If you're lost, don't ask for
> directions or use GPS. Just drive
> around forever. **Be a Man.**

This inability to admit a mistake was instilled in me at a very young age. My dad's backward thinking had the greatest effect on me. As a kid, we would be told randomly at five o'clock on a Saturday that we were going on vacation. This wasn't something that was planned out for weeks in advance with travel agencies and reservations. My father just had a premonition that it was time, so the whole family piled into the car and started driving.

Never let your wife drive. **Be a Man.**

My parents argued the entire ride as we drove up the coast. When my old man couldn't handle it anymore, he pulled off to a random hotel to try and check in. When that one had no vacancy, we would be on to the next. And the next. And the next. After a few swings and misses, we would all be loaded back into the car and headed home. No one said a word as dad's old clunker sputtered down I-95 South. Everyone in the car knew my dad was wrong to approach things this way except for him. And even if he knew he was wrong, he would never admit it, because he was a man.

When you're driving, keep your visor up and stare into the sun until you smash into something. **Be a Man.**

You're Not a Loser Until You Quit

Where I grew up we didn't learn how to work well with others; it was an "every man for himself" mentality. It wasn't until I started playing football, baseball, and hockey that I finally understood what teamwork actually was and learned about leadership, accountability, and respect. When it came to my teammates, I would have done anything for those people—they were in the trenches with me. Every team I played on was full of very different people with very different opinions but there was one thing we could all agree on: people who never practice and suffer and grind but act like they're on the team are the worst.

> Don't say "we" when talking about your favorite sports team: you don't play for them. **Be a Man.**

When you grow up without a ton of money, you quickly learn to improvise. We played street hockey with crushed cans for pucks and trash barrels flipped on their sides as the goals. We played stickball with old curtain rods and a tennis ball. Whatever it took to get the game going, we did it. These were neighborhood events too. We took over a side street and played in the middle of the road till a car was coming. This mentality wasn't just for games. We did whatever we needed to do to train as well.

> Use a hornet's nest as a speed bag. **Be a Man.**

Over the course of my life, I've been hit hard in the head a handful of times. When I was young, we didn't really know what brain injuries and concussions were. They would just say, "You got your bell rung, take five and get back out there." We thought it was normal to get back in the game before you could remember your name. Nowadays, they have done all types of research on what to do and protocols you must follow. We didn't know any better so we just handled things like it was the flu.

> Get a concussion? Sleep it off. **Be a Man.**

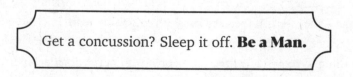

When you start getting into sports and you first experience the thrill of victory, you get hooked. We hate the idea of losing and we are always on a mission to be number one. Sometimes our love for the game spills over into real life as we look to recapture the feelings that we can only get in the heat of the battle.

> Drive around with hockey gloves on.
> If someone cuts you off, jump out of the
> car and drop your mitts. **Be a Man.**

Most people start playing sports at a young age. If they're any good, they might play all the way through high school. As my knees and hips started to shit the bed, my baseball career turned into a softball career. I stretched out my run by moving over to play first base and hitting bombs where I didn't have to leg anything out. I was never the best skater or puck handler in hockey but I could check and fight, so there was a place for me in men's leagues well into my forties. Even though my skills, my speed, and my power diminished over the years, my passion and will to win never did. Playing against kids half my age never changed the way I approached things. No matter if it was a big game or a pickup game, if you're playing against me, you're gonna get beat.

> Playing Wiffle Ball with your kids,
> strike out the side. **Be a Man.**

My dad was an avid athlete his whole life. He played baseball at the University of Miami and played racquetball and handball recreationally all the way up into his sixties. Watching him play when we were young made us all naturally want to follow in his footsteps. My brothers and I loved playing but we also loved coaching. We coached everything from Little League to varsity in everything from baseball and basketball to football and softball. A lot of these kids didn't have dads who could show them how to be a man, so we needed to play that role.

> Be a father figure to the neighborhood kids, hook up with their moms, and then disappear. **Be a Man.**

Eat Like a Man

As kids, we had a huge garden in our backyard. My Uncle Vincent would come over to the house and show us how to grow and harvest different plants so that we could eat lots of fresh fruits and vegetables and stay healthy. We grew up eating fresh deli cold cuts, imported cheeses, all different kinds of olives, and fresh-baked bread. Everything was quality or from scratch, no cutting corners in my house.

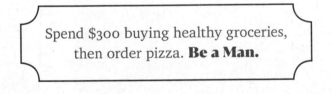

Spend $300 buying healthy groceries, then order pizza. **Be a Man.**

We ate pasta at least three to four times a week and every time we did, my mother would make it fresh that day. When it came to gravy for the pasta, we never ate anything out of a can. Everything from the tomatoes to the onions and the garlic were grown by our family. One of my favorite things to do as a little kid was dipping the bread in the gravy when my mother wasn't looking. My mother was a great cook. Her only downfall was that her hamburgers could have been used for pucks in our pond hockey games.

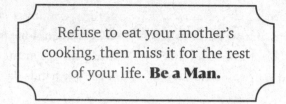

Refuse to eat your mother's cooking, then miss it for the rest of your life. **Be a Man.**

Growing up, Sunday dinner was the ultimate. People in my family rarely missed dinner but no one ever missed Sunday dinner. We ate at the same time every week and the whole family was there. My mom made homemade apple pies, Italian cookies, and ricotta pie for dessert. If I could turn back time for one thing, I think I would go back for one more meal at that table.

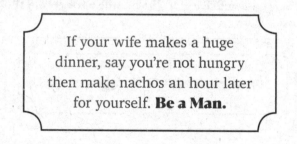

If your wife makes a huge dinner, say you're not hungry then make nachos an hour later for yourself. **Be a Man.**

When you're a teenage guy, you can pretty much eat anything you want. As long as you are staying active, you'll never gain weight. When I was in high school, I used to go to the sub shop with my buddy. We'd order a large of every sub they had on the menu and two large pizzas and eat it all, just the two of us. Then I would go to my girlfriend's house afterward and eat again.

If you order a six-foot sub, eat the whole thing yourself. **Be a Man.**

As I tried to stay in good shape into my twenties, I cut down on the grains and started eating like a real caveman. I ate red meat, beef, lamb, bison, venison, and elk. We were always around people who hunted so we ate whatever we could get our hands on.

If it's not meat, it's not a meal. **Be a Man.**

When it came to eating meat, I was never one to avoid the fat. Some people will trim it all off and reduce a huge piece of juicy steak down to only a couple of bites. I was always taught that the fat is where the flavor hides. I would eat the whole thing and spit out the bones.

Eat a hunk of meat with your bare hands like an animal. **Be a Man.**

When it comes to drinking, it's usually one of two things: beer or water. Water is my day drink. I'm working out, staying hydrated, and keeping my energy up. Some people walk around with a twenty-ounce water bottle, but I always walk around with a gallon in my hand. Beer is my recovery drink. I found out recently that the flavonoids in hops in beer can increase muscle mass by preventing tissue breakdown during inactivity. So it looks like I'm not stopping beer any time soon.

Drink one beer . . . then drink another one . . . and another one. **Be a Man.**

When I was young, there was no diet culture. Guys didn't talk about their weight and what they needed to work on. You dealt with shit internally and you figured it out or you died, like a man. These days, every asshole talks about dieting every two fucking minutes. There is no worse guy in the world than the guy who is only five pounds overweight and complaining about how he needs to lose weight, probably to a guy who needs to lose fifty pounds.

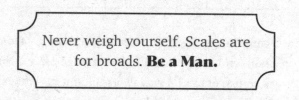

Never weigh yourself. Scales are for broads. **Be a Man.**

Once we figure out that diets don't work, we will be a lot better off. No one has ever stayed on a diet. They do it for a week or a month or a year, and then fall back when something goes wrong in life. If we want to change anything, we need to change everything.

Never go on a diet. Eat whatever you want, whenever you want. **Be a Man.**

Gym Rat

For the past forty years, I've been frequenting gyms all over the country. Wherever I was, whatever I was doing for work, I always made time for the gym. That's why I can still snap a twenty-five-year-old in half today. If I could go back in time and change one thing, it would be that I went to the gym *even more*, and got in really great shape.

> Spend more time in the gym than around your family. **Be a Man.**

My first gym experience was a makeshift setup I had in the corner of my basement when I was ten years old. I had those cheap, crappy plastic weights with sand in them and I used random pipes that I found in the room to do military presses. One day, I snapped the pipe that was used to keep the basement door locked from the inside in half. When my dad asked about it, I immediately denied the entire thing so I didn't get my ass whooped. When it came to updating our setup, we were always snooping around the boxing club down the street and looking in the neighborhood trash for new additions.

> Go to the beach and work out
> with boulders. **Be a Man.**

From high school and into college, I started really going hard. Recreational sports were getting more and more popular and gym culture was gaining steam. Gyms went from garage and basement setups to strip malls and then huge warehouses. This was around the time everyone had big hair, both the guys and the girls. All the women were sporting shoulder pads and almost everyone was wearing tiny shorts with neon tank tops. This trend lasted most of the 1980s until there were just too many incidents of random junk popping out.

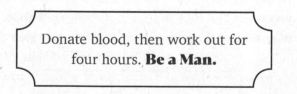

> Donate blood, then work out for
> four hours. **Be a Man.**

In the 1980s, anabolic steroid use broke out from bodybuilding competitions and seeped into the general population. Guys everywhere were trying steroids out as a way to get fit quickly and impress broads. Tons of guys I knew were shooting needles in their asses to get ripped. Most times, it inflated your biceps and your ego and deflated your balls and your patience. The people that were shooting steroids were always on edge and just one move away from a rage incident.

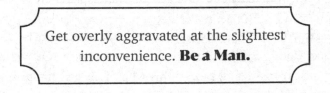

Get overly aggravated at the slightest inconvenience. **Be a Man.**

In the mid-1980s, any steroid you wanted could be bought for super cheap. People were mixing doses and brands, creating a super cocktail for muscle and destruction. It wasn't until 1988 that their sale even became illegal so in the early to mid-1980s, it was a free-for-all in gyms across America. You would see deals going down in the locker room daily.

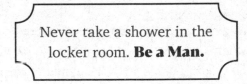

Never take a shower in the locker room. **Be a Man.**

The craziest thing I ever saw in the gym was a bench-clearing brawl over a steroid deal gone wrong. One day I was posted up doing a chest workout when I saw a few of the big guys arguing near the free weights, something about this guy ripped off that guy, and so on. One of them threw the other into a ten-foot mirror and the glass shattered everywhere. He peeled himself off the floor all bloody, crawled to the free weights, and gunned a twenty-pound dumbbell off the other guy's head. They ran at each other, grappled, and rolled all over the floor as all the 'roid heads jumped in and started throwing haymakers. That was a fun workout.

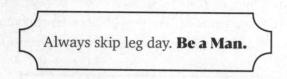

Always skip leg day. **Be a Man.**

There are levels to the gym experience. You can be the guy who's just doing lightweight reps, trying to stay fit. Or you can be the guy just tryna get away from his wife. This guy hangs out near the water bubbler and hops on the treadmill for an hour so he can watch the baseball game in peace. You can even be the guy who takes it super seriously and goes hard every time.

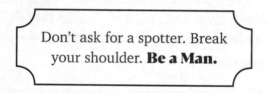

Don't ask for a spotter. Break your shoulder. **Be a Man.**

For me, the gym has always been a place where I can sort problems out. So when someone pissed me off at work or I got into an argument with my girl, I could go to the gym and clear my head. If I don't go to the gym five days a week, I turn into a maniac ready to rip someone's head off.

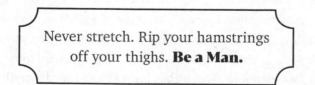

Never stretch. Rip your hamstrings off your thighs. **Be a Man.**

Playing the Field

In my parents' generation, dating was a lot different. You met a broad, you met her family, and then you got married. Most times, these couples barely knew each other. Before you knew it, they had five kids together.

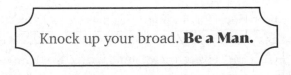

Knock up your broad. **Be a Man.**

The next forty years of their lives were an unholy combination of miscommunication, an unwillingness to understand each other, and the complete absence of sex or any kind of emotional or physical affection. These couples would stay together and keep their cold war going until they died or until the kids were finally old enough to handle the divorce.

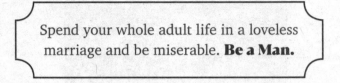

> Spend your whole adult life in a loveless marriage and be miserable. **Be a Man.**

By the time I was in my early twenties, the world was completely different from the one I had grown up with. People were trying different things. The idea of meeting people to date in random places began a new chapter toward finding what was actually out there. It might have been a vast improvement over marrying the first girl you got to third base with, but this method still had its flaws.

> F*ck this internet dating shit. Meet a broad the old-fashioned way: at a bar or at a funeral. **Be a Man.**

Our expectations for finding "the perfect woman" have been heavily exaggerated through books, TV, and movies. We are told that the perfect girl is out there somewhere, her hair in curlers, staring at the phone, waiting just for you. But she isn't because she doesn't exist and she never will. Sure, falling in love feels like hitting the lottery, but not because you're gonna be rich and happy and totally set for the rest of your days. Finding the right girl feels like hitting the lottery because what you are doing is gambling.

> If you feel like your girl might be a crazy train wreck who will ruin your life, get her name tattooed on you. **Be a Man.**

Dating around is smaller stakes than falling in love but it's still a numbers game. The house always wins eventually . . . but the more you play, the greater your chances of hitting it big. Think about it like baseball. The more pitches you see, the more hits you're gonna get. When it comes to dating, more is always better. Not all dates are going to go well. Sometimes, you need to run away as fast as you can.

> Forget your girl's birthday, and when she asks what you got her, tell her it's in the car. Go outside, then leave. **Be a Man.**

One of the most unforgettable dates I've ever had was at one of America's most iconic stadiums, Fenway Park. If you have never been there, it is a hot, wet shoe box dropped right into the middle of the city. It has a certain nostalgic charm and the fans are always loyal and intense. But Fenway is known for its not just intimate, but cramped, seating. They jam pack 37,000 people on top of each other for every home game. Although they have cleaned it up quite a bit over the years, in the 1980s it was a real shithole. But the men's bathrooms were infamous for their piss holes—their signature trough urinals.

> When you're at a public urinal, stare straight ahead at the wall. **Be a Man.**

Every time you entered the bathrooms at Fenway, a different adventure presented itself, but pissing into the trough urinals was like no other feeling in the world. You were urinating shoulder to shoulder with grown men and teenagers and old-timers, who looked like they were about to keel over and die, with no divider of any kind. Everyone was drunk, swearing and leaning on the guy next to them. The drains were filled with gum, piss, spit, and cigarette butts. They even had a piss trough in the middle of the room so guys could piss on both sides of it. You'd be facing another guy pissing and you could just look up and make eye contact if that was your thing. It kinda made you feel like every one of those men at the urinal was your brother, and that all your brothers were about to lose their balance and piss up your leg.

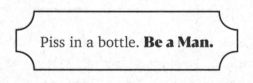

Piss in a bottle. **Be a Man.**

Anyway, my date was on a hot summer night. I parked near Fenway, and walked to State Street to meet up with this voluptuous broad I had met a few days earlier. We hopped on the subway to Kenmore Square and pulled up right before game time. She had come right from work so she was still dressed in a skirt and high heels, not exactly the best attire for drinking and baseball. She said she had a tough day and needed a drink. So, instantly, she was speaking my language. We stepped into the Cask 'n Flagon for a few beers, then headed into the game. Once we got in, I was focused on finding our seats but she insisted that we find another beer stand before sitting down. We both loaded up, double fisting, and headed down to our seats on the third baseline.

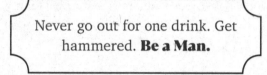

Never go out for one drink. Get hammered. **Be a Man.**

After the first half inning, she said she needed to take a piss. I stayed in our seats shooting the shit with some people next to us. Ten minutes later, she was back with a tray full of beers. I've been around some broads that can drink in my day but rarely do you find women that are really initiating the action. Just like clockwork, every inning she said she needed to piss and came back with a full tray like a waitress.

After about five innings, the Sox were down 4–0 but I was feeling pretty good. She left for yet another four-pack. A few minutes later, I heard the crowd launch into its biggest roar of the night and I whipped my head back toward the aisle. It was almost like time had stopped. This broad's high heel had snapped and, in slow motion, her beer tray flew up in the air. She flailed her arms and started falling down the aisle. The beers flew up in slow motion and then came down real fast, drenching a family of four. She tumbled down the steps, then landed face-first on some guys a few rows behind me.

I ran back there like Kevin Costner in *The Bodyguard* and peeled her off of some random dude's crotch. Somehow, miraculously, she was totally fine. When I got her back to the seats, she wasn't embarrassed at all, just upset that she had wasted the beers. By this point, I knew I was dealing with a different type of broad. I figured she'd want to go home and get cleaned up so I asked her if she wanted to leave. She said, "Yeah, let's go hit up a bar on Lansdowne."

We had a wild night that ended sometime the next day but this ended up being the first and last time we ever hung out. It's good to party and have fun, but if she parties harder than you, proceed with caution.

FIVE BEST PLACES TO PICK UP BROADS

1. **WALKING THE DOG.** After the companionship, the best part of owning a dog is the way they magnetically attract girls. This method is foolproof because you don't have to do any of the work. Literally the only thing you have to do is take your dog for a walk. The dog breaks the ice and does all the heavy lifting. Just try not to have a hot handful of fresh dog turds in a thin plastic bag while your dream girl approaches, OK?

2. **THE GYM.** If you are into getting in shape, the best place to find people trying the same is here.

Plus it eliminates step one of trying to figure out what she's into. Worst-case scenario, you get a workout in, you fat lazy tub of guts.

3. **THE SUPERMARKET.** You need to be confident when talking to a broad in the produce section or this isn't going to end well for you. If you are nervous, you just look like a creep sneaking up behind her. Don't open with eggplants or cucumbers or zucchini, you degenerate. Ask her for some advice on avocados, literally anything about the avocados. Broads are crazy for avocados, I can't figure it out, but it's true.

4. **ON A PLANE.** When you are stuck sitting next to a pretty girl for the next three hours with people walking around and serving you drinks, this is a great opportunity to spice up the conversation. After a couple Johnny Walker doubles, all the fear and doubt slip away. By the time you land, it's almost like you've already had your first date. Hell, she may just invite you home.

5. **IN PLAIN SIGHT.** There are always new women and opportunities right in front of your face. Open your fucking eyes.

Heading to the Disco

I've never been much of a trendsetter but I've always been a tone setter. Any time you walk into a room as a man, it's in our nature for our presence to be felt, whether it's consciously or not. We walk in making grunts with each step, knocking over a chair, or bumping into a waitress. We just want everyone to know that we're there. Over the years, I've been in a scuffle or two. For me, it was never about jumping in late or retaliating. I liked to establish the mood.

If you're in a bar brawl, smash a bottle on your head and set the tone. **Be a Man.**

When I was in my twenties, I worked as a bouncer at a club on Revere Beach and over at The Palace. In the 1980s and early 1990s, The Palace was a poor man's Studio 54. It was like a legendary New York–style dance club but on Route 1, north of Boston. The space was sixty thousand square feet with six different clubs inside, all playing different music for different crowds. There was a huge wrap-around staircase that seemed like it was the length of a football field. Like clockwork, every night at 2:00 A.M. the girls in high heels would tumble down the stairs after too many cocktails.

> If your girl gets drunk at the bar, get her a water and keep drinking on her tab. **Be a Man.**

This place had a little of something for everyone. On any given night there could be a Hawaiian Tropic bikini contest in one room and a concert with up-and-coming pop singers in another. For the ladies, there was a regular show called "Male Encounters." This was a favorite destination for local bachelorette parties.

Every week, DJs came from all around the world to set the tone for a full spectrum of different dance parties. The Palace was the best place to pick up women. You got a few drinks, you danced a few songs, and it was a wrap. By drinking and dancing the first time you meet someone, you really speed up the process of getting to know them. Sometimes you stayed till the final bell. Other times, you dipped out quick to side-step a clinger.

> Dip out on your tab and forget your
> credit card at the bar. **Be a Man.**

Over the years working the door, we broke up our fair share of scuffles and melees. On a typical night, it was me and one other guy working. One night, the bouncer working with me was jawing back and forth with a customer, trying to escort him out the door. The customer took a swing at him and a fight broke out in the front hallway and quickly spilled into the parking lot.

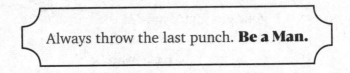

> Always throw the last punch. **Be a Man.**

I jumped in the middle to try to break it up. A guy was coming up behind my friend and trying to grab his arms. Just as I lunged to stop him, I got hit from the side with a haymaker. My jaw snapped back—I felt like I got hit by Mike Tyson. I saw stars for a second and stumbled down to one knee. I've never been hit so hard in my entire life.

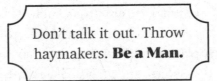

> Don't talk it out. Throw
> haymakers. **Be a Man.**

When I got my bearings right and the scuffle had diminished, I found out I had actually been hit by the woman whose boyfriend was going toe-to-toe with the other bouncer. I ran into the lady years later. We had a laugh about it over a beer.

Get in a brawl with strangers, then get wasted with them the rest of the night. **Be a Man.**

The Last of the Romantics

Never be romantic. **Be a Man.**

Romance to women is all about attention to detail, communication, and having a man who is pleasantly unpredictable. By nature, men have always been unpredictable, but it's not always in the most gratifying of ways. When a woman covers the bed in rose petals for a romantic evening celebrating her guy's birthday, he comes home shitfaced from the bar after pounding birthday shots with the boys. When a woman plans for a late-night champagne kiss for New Year's Eve, her man starts snoring at 9:00 P.M. after working doubles all week.

> Buy your girl's Valentine's Day presents at a gas station. **Be a Man.**

Women want us to text as soon as we get to the destination. They want us to hug them right when we come in the door. Women want us to bring them flowers for no reason, just because. We have a hard time doing a lot of these things because we are extremely disconnected from the emotions of appreciation, gratitude, excitement, and love. We were raised to do the opposite in most cases. The only emotions most men are capable of feeling are hunger, thirst, and exhaustion. Don't get me wrong, some aspects of romance come easy to us. Men are usually really good at not trying too hard and giving their partner lots and lots of space.

> When your girl gets home, don't ask her anything about her day. **Be a Man.**

There are many areas of intimate connection where we really struggle. Our resistance to romance is so deeply ingrained that it would take decades to dismantle it. Romance takes patience and vulnerability and communication, being able to apologize when you make mistakes and forgive mistakes of your significant other, and embracing small but meaningful gestures like holding hands in public.

THREE COMMON WAYS TO EXPRESS YOUR LOVE

1. Put the game on and ignore her.

2. Never apologize, you didn't do it.

3. Never hold hands with your broad.

When it comes to eating, men rarely see going out as a romantic occasion. We are cavemen—when we are hungry we stuff food in our faces until we are full. We don't care where we go, as long as they serve drinks and there is a TV with sports on somewhere in the room so we can watch, looking over our girl's shoulder.

When you are supposed to go on a romantic dinner with your girl, invite all your boys. **Be a Man.**

If you decide that this is the one, the broad you can't go on living your life without, it's time to shoot your shot. Remember that the proposal is extremely important to broads. This is when the woman wants you to be the most romantic you have ever been or will ever be. They want this to be a story out of a fairy tale that they can tell their friends and family for years to come. It should be magical, it should be mind-blowing, but most importantly, it should be unexpected. Don't disappoint.

> Propose to your girl while she's taking a shit. **Be a Man.**

Cook Like a Man

In the 1950s and 1960s, the women ran the kitchen. Every meal from breakfast to dinner was prepared, cooked, delivered, and cleaned up by our mothers. The only time our dads set foot in the kitchen was to get a beer out of the fridge or rip a leg off the turkey on the stove.

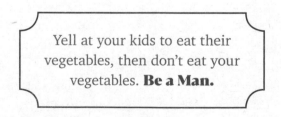

Yell at your kids to eat their vegetables, then don't eat your vegetables. **Be a Man.**

By the time we grew up and moved out, things were already a lot different. People weren't getting married by eighteen anymore so we had to start figuring things out a little differently than our dads did. We didn't have a new bride at home who was locked away in the kitchen slaving over a stove all day. We needed to cook for ourselves.

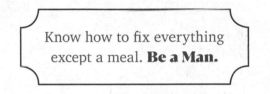

Know how to fix everything except a meal. **Be a Man.**

This led to some of the worst meals known to mankind. We didn't know what the fuck we were doing, we would mix whatever we had in the fridge and make it into a burrito. I found myself skipping meals for the first time in my life because I couldn't stand to eat my own food.

If you cook something and it's terrible, eat the whole thing. **Be a Man.**

As I mentioned, we never used canned food when I was young. But when I started living on my own, eating canned goods and vegetables sounded like a good idea to cut down on my prep time. I bought a shit ton of canned goods and threw them in my pantry. At this point, I had spent so little time in the kitchen I had no idea what a can opener was. So one night when I was drunk and there was no food in the house, I started pulling cans out of the pantry. After failing to figure out how to jar loose the contents inside, I started beating the cans with a hammer to get into them.

> If you try something and it doesn't work, hit it with a hammer. **Be a Man.**

FIVE GO-TO MEALS

1. **RAMEN SANDWICH.** Open a package of ramen, run it under hot water for five seconds, sprinkle the seasoning packet on top, and ta-da, now it's a sandwich.

2. **TONIGHT'S SPECIAL.** Take a tortilla, spread on some ketchup and grated cheese, and pop it in the oven for ten minutes. Boom—makeshift pizza.

3. **PROTEIN SHAKE.** Mix a raw egg in with a beer.

4. **CHEF'S SALAD.** Pour a V8 into a beer and stir it with a Slim Jim—now it's a Chef's Salad.

5. **MAMA'S DELIGHT.** Take a drive over to your mother's house and drop in around dinnertime "for a visit."

Living with Your Broad: Weathering the Storm

When we live alone, we live like absolute animals. We eat the same meal every night, we do laundry once every three months, and we never change the sheets on the bed. When we are in a relationship, we are supposed to change from knuckle-dragging sub-humans to modern men, about two million years of evolution in maybe two weeks if you're lucky.

Never let a broad pick out your clothes. **Be a Man.**

The older we get, there are fewer and fewer things we can call our own, especially once we commit to a serious relationship. We take the little space we have extremely seriously. Sheds, garages, and basements become our sanctuaries where we build things, watch sports, and break balls with the boys. The places where we store our tools, hide our possessions, and keep our beers cold become comforting caves of solitude.

Don't buy a bed. Sleep on the floor. **Be a Man.**

Any time you move in with a broad, make sure you have a place you can retreat to or your relationship won't last very long. When we catch that first whiff of strawberry potpourri or her "Autumn Wreath" Yankee Candle, we'll sleep better knowing we have a bomb shelter we can retreat to when we finally hit the breaking point. No matter how big or small it is, a bunker safe from your broad is essential to survival. This is a place where you can throw socks on the floor, leave half-empty beers, and let last week's nachos grow a beard of black mold without nagging comments and ridicule. This disgusting den is the only place she won't set foot in and for one reason: she's afraid of what is living behind those walls. Don't be ashamed of your filth . . . own it!

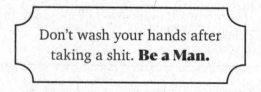

Don't wash your hands after taking a shit. **Be a Man.**

The toughest part of taking your relationship from casual dating to actually living together is dealing with the reality behind a person's avatar. When they're just getting to know someone new, people tend to put out a version of themselves that they think other people will like. We think this walking résumé will make such a great impression that the other person might want to actually have sex with us. The problem is that once we have secured the bag we revert to our animalistic roots.

Sure, this dating technique works, but it can create a real sticky situation down the line. The major problem is the backlash of reality. When the real world catches up to us, we're gonna realize we've created these unattainable expectations. Now the other person is going to hold us to a new standard that we will never live up to. Sure, she looks great and smells great at the bar and you managed to put on clean jeans and even deodorant. Then six months later you're sitting on opposite ends of the couch, hungover and fat and miserable, farting into your sweatpants, watching *American Idol*, and wondering how the fuck you got here. If, at this point, you know it's not going to work, get out as fast as you can.

> Move in with your girl to speed up the breakup. **Be a Man.**

I moved in with a broad once and it barely lasted three days. We were arguing from the moment we woke up to the moment we both passed out from exhaustion. You can get along with someone just fine but once you move in together, it's a totally different ball game.

It was the second night and we decided to have a few drinks and make dinner together. She was heating up some olive oil in a skillet on the stove, ready to sauté up some onions and garlic. Like clockwork, she made a slick comment. Like clockwork, I countered with a venomous comeback. She took the shoe off her foot and gunned it at my head, then bee-lined it out the front door, slamming it behind her with a bang. I was so furious that I ran after her, slamming the door behind me with a bang. *Wait. Fuck, was it locked?* I immediately turned around and rattled the knob. *Fuck, it was locked!* I could barely see through the frosted glass on the front door but when a huge oil-based flame shot up from the skillet and caught the ceiling on fire in the kitchen, yeah, there was no question what was happening—the entire place was about to burn down.

I ran around the house to check the first-floor windows, but they were all locked. After a couple of long, desperate minutes, she showed back up.

"What's going on?" she screamed.

"What does it look like? The fucking house is on fire!"

We ran around to the side of the house and I lifted her onto my shoulders so she could check the tops of the windows. We were running out of time. Finally, when we got to the bedroom, the top part was unlocked and she slid it down. Dark black smoke bellowed out of the window as she jumped off my shoulders through the window and into the house. She crawled to the front door and let me in. The smoke punched me in the face as I ran into the hallway toward the kitchen to try and put this thing out. I couldn't see a foot in front of me and I was knocking shit over as I made my way to the kitchen. When I finally got in there, I grabbed something off a chair and used it to extinguish the inferno. Turns out it was her favorite jacket—whoops.

The entire interior had a thick black oily film on it. We turned every fan in the place on high to air out the house for the rest of the night. We stayed up till four in the morning, repainting all of the cabinets and ceilings. When we were finally done, I offered to let her take a shower first, and she said thanks, the first sincere thing she'd said since we moved in. By the time she was out, I was long gone.

Move out in the middle of the night. **Be a Man.**

Do It Yourself

When it comes to car repairs, moving, or going away on a vacation, the best way to do it is always alone. Sure, it's easier to just drop the car off at the mechanic but it feels like every time we do, we get screwed. Sure, a helping hand would be great to move that couch or your 200-pound solid oak dresser, but do you really want them to hold that favor over your head? I know a weekend with the family could be fun, but would you actually have time to relax with all those people around?

> Don't go to a mechanic, just watch YouTube videos. **Be a Man.**

Being a trailblazer isn't for everyone. Doing everything by yourself isn't easy. But the beauty of being totally independent is that, when the work is done, you will never owe anyone jack shit.

> If you have to lift up something heavy, don't ask for any help. Throw your back out. **Be a Man.**

There is no more annoying trait in men than being needy. I'm sure you have friends or acquaintances whom you haven't talked to in months who call you up to help move a couch or put the hardtop on their Jeep. These are not men. Instead of asking for help, instead of accepting help when it was offered, a real man would throw his neck out trying to put the hardtop on alone. Then when trying to balance it, he would watch that stupid expensive hardtop slide off and smash to the ground.

> Move a couch down three flights of stairs by yourself. **Be a Man.**

Some might label you as hardheaded or stubborn for doing something by yourself that should have been done by a team of people. But the time it takes to call someone, wait for them, and then have them disappoint you when they can't even carry their side . . . you're better off just taking chances on your own.

I would rather watch YouTube tutorials, struggle on my back in the dirt to change out ball joints, and complain about it all day than get ripped off for forty dollars. When you do something you didn't know you had in you, when you pull off the impossible, there is no better feeling. But if you can't do it, if you try and fail, there is only one other thing that can make you feel better.

> Can't fix something? Chuck a fucking wrench across the room. **Be a Man.**

THE FIVE ULTIMATE DIY PROJECTS

1. **HIDING CORDS.** There is nothing more annoying than seeing rogue wires sticking out randomly below the new TV that you just mounted on the wall. You can wear the same jeans for two weeks straight but the thought of a visible wire will make any man blow a fuse. I don't care if you have to chisel through concrete, hide the damn cords.

2. **BUILD A KEGERATOR.** The idea of an ice-cold keg doling out perfectly crisp draft beers in the comfort of your own home is something that puts a fire in every man's heart. We all know how much fun keg parties were—now you can have one for breakfast.

3. **MAKE A TIRE COFFEE TABLE.** Most guys have at least one random tire kicking around in the backyard. If you need a good place to put your drinks and kick up your legs, stack a couple of tires and then build a top. Your wife is gonna love it.

4. **FIRE PIT TOP.** Men love spending time around the fire but what about those times when it's too hot outside? Time to transform it into the ultimate table. Now everyone's favorite trip and fall fire hazard can hold snacks and beers.

5. **BUILD THE ULTIMATE OUTDOOR KITCHEN.** Women love to say that they run the house, and that's fine. But when it comes to outdoor cooking, we've got it under control. Men don't want anything to do with the kitchen in the house but building an outdoor

kitchen provides us with endless possibilities to cook what we want, when we want, how we want, naked and drunk if we want. Then we always have a place to hang out, especially on nice summer nights. Preferably alone.

Self-Care

I've always said a man should keep his mind clear, focused, and as stress-free as possible. Stress is caused by all types of shit, from money problems to health issues to bad relationships with broads. When all that stress overwhelms us, we become angry, irritable, depressed, and anxious assholes.

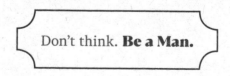

Don't think. **Be a Man.**

Any time I've gotten stressed out over the years, it's because I let little things build up when I should have just knocked 'em out of the box. Sure, going to the gym or hitting the heavy bag can be a good way to get some aggression out but it's not going to solve everything. Sometimes we need to figure out what's holding us back and face it head-on.

> Look in the mirror. If you don't like what you see, stop looking. **Be a Man.**

In true male fashion, most times we're moving so fast that we don't make time to enjoy anything. We wake up, go to work, grind all day long, and then come home exhausted. We're tired so we eat something quick, then turn on the TV. We look at our phones for an hour, have a couple of drinks, and pass out sitting up on the couch. Then the next day, we wake up and do it all over again. It's easy to get caught up in this cycle and feel like there are just not enough hours in the day. Most of the guys I know are doing stuff for everyone else all the time and they don't put any effort into taking care of themselves. No matter if you have a big family or you live at home by yourself, making time to get away from everyone to listen to some music or get in a workout isn't selfish, it's essential.

> Meditation is scientifically proven to help both your body and your mind. Never do it. **Be a man.**

Self-care isn't just taking care of your body and your mind, it's everything, the whole package. Most guys don't know that the largest organ in your body is your skin. When's the last time you did anything to take care of your skin? It's gotta last you your whole life and it's the first thing anyone sees.

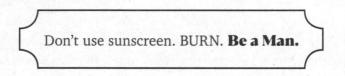

Don't use sunscreen. BURN. **Be a Man.**

Vanity is something we all battle with on a daily basis, whether we want to admit it or not. No one likes the guy who wants to be showered in attention for running a mile or wants to be praised like a hero for losing the ten pounds he gains every holiday season. On the other side of the coin, we don't like watching our physical appearance go down the shitter either. In our twenties, we're bulletproof—nobody ever looked as good as we do and we're gonna live forever. In our thirties, things start to slow down a tiny bit but we're still hanging in there. After thirty-five, our natural good looks start to fall off. After forty, the cracks really start to show. If you're not married by now, it's basically over because you have become the Old Creep. Are you fat *and* skinny? You have a dad bod even though you don't have kids? You have the build of a detective who's been on a stakeout for twenty years and you're trying to hide this mess with a pair of wraparound shades? It's not working, bro, it's not working at all. You may as well get a bunch of cats. When you find yourself turning into the Old Creep, you have only two choices: take it in stride or throw a Hail Mary.

Hot yoga's for girls. Wanna try and lose weight? Take a hot shit. **Be a Man.**

If we're eating cookies, cranking cigarettes, pounding alcohol, baking in the sun, and not sleeping, the years start to catch up quick. By forty-five we look fifty-five, by fifty-five we look seventy, and by sixty-five we look dead. These are probably all things we should take into consideration, but we love something sweet after something salty, we love a smoke after a meal, we love a few drinks to take the edge off, we don't like the hassle of slathering cream on our face before going out in sun, and we really don't like the idea of going to bed early and missing out on the action.

> Go everywhere, do everything, never take pictures, don't remember a damn thing. **Be a Man.**

For me, self-care always has something to do with being mentally prepared. I've always leaned on routine and structure to help me to relax. Every weekend, I like to set up my entire week, from work schedule to family time and hanging out with friends. But my favorite things of all are usually done by myself. I love taking cruises on my boat off the coast of Gloucester, Mass. When I'm not on the boat, I like driving aimlessly around up and down the coast or watching old hockey fights on VHS.

> Protect your relationships with your friends and family. Spend all your time alone. **Be a Man.**

GROOMING TIPS

TAKE CARE OF YOUR TEETH

When you're a kid, your parents preach constantly about the havoc that eating junk food wreaks on your body and the importance of brushing and flossing your teeth when you wake up and before you go to bed. Parents hit that so hard because they know it's a losing battle. Even though this act of cleanliness takes only a few minutes twice a day, we convince ourselves that we don't have that kind of time. Many men treat brushing their teeth like they do washing their clothes: they'll get to it when they get to it. But when you rip the crotch out of your jeans or your favorite Steve Miller T-shirt stinks constantly of sweat, you can get new ones. You get one set of teeth to last you your whole adult life so this minor bit of maintenance is essential. Not brushing your teeth is one grooming fail that can have real complications in a relationship too, as your garbage disposal of a mouth is what they need to kiss.

Never brush your teeth. Be a Man.

THE KEY TO GREAT HAIR

When we are young, we all seem to have a thick, healthy crop of lettuce on our head. We pay no attention to it, we rarely wash it, we toss it under a greasy ball cap that only comes off when we sleep, and we only cut it when we need to go to a funeral or a wedding or court date. The plush hair of a young man probably has to do with the fact that we live stress-free lives up to the age of about twenty-two. When romantic relationships start creeping in and the real world grabs us by the balls, we see more and more of our hair in the shower drain. Suddenly we start paying tons of attention to hair products and diets and bogus snake oil hair loss cure-alls in hopes we might be able to hold on to our manly manes. We can't go back to the stress-free life of a teenager so we are better off just not giving a shit about our gleaming domes, and owning our fate. Stop throwing your money away on all that garbage and just go back to what you did when your hair was growing like a weed.

Wash your hair with a bar of soap. Be a Man.

THE MAN'S GUIDE TO SKIN CARE

Women love to make skin care a ritual. They wash their faces multiple times a day; they wear mud masks, apply creams and serums; they moisturize and exfoliate. The only time I even splash water on my face is when I'm super hungover and

I'm trying everything to pull it together. For me, it's really too much work to apply and protect. Fuck it. If lose some skin, I can make more.

> If you have skin cancer, don't see a doctor, get a belt sander and remove it yourself.
> Be a Man.

OLD MAN BACK

Men seem to have back pain from the time we are little kids. This is probably due to many contributing factors but mostly because of our reckless nature. We love to lift heavy shit without stretching and never use proper form. We sit at work in the same broken-down chairs for five hours at a time and barely move. We sleep in the most fucked-up positions possible. Our doctors recommend surgery, our kids bring us Advil, our wives beg us to try yoga, Pilates, acupuncture, anything. But when it comes to men's back pain, there's only one way to deal with it.

> When your back hurts, don't do anything to fix it, just bitch about it constantly.
> Be a Man.

The Relationship Center

KNOW WHEN TO HOLD 'EM, KNOW WHEN TO FOLD 'EM

Over the years, I've been in my fair share of interesting relationships with varying levels of common interests. Sometimes you both like to party, other times you both like working out. Maybe you just like going out for Vietnamese food and drinking mai tais. But it's not your shared love of basket weaving or air hockey or mixed martial arts (MMA) that's going to keep you together. It's not even mind-blowing sex—that has a shelf life—or true love that's going to make your relationship last. The real reason men stay in relationships is because we have nothing better to do. When you have only one option, hey, that's your best option. But when you're stuck in a bad relationship with someone you can't stand, there is no worse feeling in the world. Sometimes nothing is better than something, and it's just time to hit the road.

> Tell your broad you're going to the store for booze and butts and never come home. **Be a Man.**

We have all made the mistake of completely misreading a situation, thinking someone is a good fit, and then winding up in a relationship with some gold-digging, shoplifting, drama-farming psychopath. OK, let's be honest, when it comes to broads, men are never gonna learn to make better decisions. But even if men are never gonna get smart enough to stay out of the honeypot, we can improve our exit strategies. The more you play the game, the better you get at spotting the signs that you're headed into a tailspin, and the better you get at recognizing when it's finally time to bounce. Knowing how to read the signs can help to eliminate wasted time and speed up the process. That way you can quietly move out when she's having frozen strawberry margaritas with the girls instead of waiting past the point of no return like a chump and coming home after work one day to find all your shit out in the street.

Below are some telltale signs that you have messed up and will have to change your phone number again.

SHE COMES ON TOO STRONG, TOO EARLY

This is something you'll notice a few weeks in, by which point it will be too late. If she's laying it on thick and constantly talking about your future together but you barely know her, it's time to go. Don't wait for her to come home with a tramp stamp with your name, retreat and exit immediately.

> If she sends you a long heartfelt
> text, pouring out her feelings . . .
> reply back K. **Be a Man.**

SHE'S OBSESSED WITH SOCIAL MEDIA

I mean, if it's Be a Man videos, that's one thing. But if she's obsessed with details of other people's lives, she is very quickly going to become obsessed with the details of your life before she met you. You're about to get interrogated about every relationship you ever had before her, down to Marcy, the girl up the block who wrote your name on her notebook with hearts around it when you were in third grade. Don't wait for the hammer to fall, run away as fast as you can.

> Tell your girl to stop pretending you're doing big things on social media. Your life isn't that great. **Be a Man.**

SHE'S JEALOUS AND CONTROLLING

This never works out for anyone. Respecting your broad is one thing but if there is a big playoff game, I'm going to watch it with the boys. If she burns more than three jerseys or keys your truck more than once, don't wait for her to exceed the deductible, hit the bricks.

> Tell her you're going over to your buddies' for an hour, then walk in the door the next morning and ask her what's for breakfast. **Be a Man.**

SHE'S A BOOZE BAG

Listen, I like to have fun just as much as the next guy. And I have nothing but respect for a girl who can keep up with the boys. But if she's drinking you under the table every night, there's a problem. Do you really want to wake up on a Tuesday morning to your broad snoring on the couch, a piece of pizza cheese on her chest, and her high heels in the neighbor's front yard? If the majority of your late nights are drama-filled nightmares, spent arguing and dodging red Solo cups, it's time to call yourself an Uber and get the fuck out of there. If you're enough of a dumbass that you already shacked up with her, just wait to move out when she gets locked up for her next DUI.

> If your girlfriend wants to drink, only let her have one. **Be a Man.**

SHE DOESN'T GET ALONG WITH FAMILY AND HAS NO FRIENDS

You can tell a lot about a person by how well they get along with the people closest to them. Everyone has gripes with their folks but somehow we find a way to get along well enough to stay in the will and maybe even get invited home for Thanksgiving. If your broad has daddy issues, that may mean she has low expectations for you, so congrats, you have found the woman of your dreams. But if your broad has a fractured relationship with her mother, that's a huge red flag. If she doesn't talk to either of her parents and has no friends,

best-case scenario, she turned state's evidence and ratted out someone and is now in the Federal Witness Protection Program. It might
be time to throw another line in the water.

> If you're in a big argument with your girl,
> call her by her mother's name. **Be a Man.**

Not every relationship is a bad one. There are times when you
actually get along with someone and you have fun together.
If she checks all the boxes, hold on to what you got.

☐ SHE'S LOYAL. I'm from a city where the Red Sox didn't win
a World Series for eighty-six years but Sox fans never lost faith.
Of course, if your broad sticks around for eighty-six years, you'll
have a different problem on your hands, but we'll burn that
bridge when we come to it.

☐ SHE DOESN'T BREED DRAMA. Life is sufficiently full of
drama, you don't need a broad who feels the need to manufac-
ture more of it.

☐ SHE'S DOWN TO CHILL AT HOME. Yeah, it's nice to have
a broad that's willing to tie one on occasionally, maybe run wild
in Mexico together for a weekend. But if you haven't run out of
gas yet, you will soon. Make sure you wind up with someone
down to hang on the couch for long periods of time. If she gets
antsy and wants to get up to grab you another beer or maybe
some nachos, that's fine.

- NO PRESSURE. A good broad is like a good pair of boxer briefs: supportive but not constricting. If she's cutting off the blood flow, let her go.

- SHE'S TRUSTWORTHY. I'm not saying all your guy friends are creeps and perverts and degenerates but hey, they hang around with you so they are probably all creeps and perverts and degenerates. As long as you can trust your girl, you can still hang out with guys nicknamed Killer.

- YOUR FAMILY LIKES HER. If your mother loves your broad, she may become so obsessed with your broad's birthday that maybe she'll forget about yours and you can actually enjoy that day for once.

- SHE LOVES HER FAMILY. If your broad still loves her family, she'll spend lots of time with them and less time with you and that is the secret to a long successful relationship.

And if after all that, you think you found a good one, remember . . .

> If you're in love, don't shout it from the rooftops. Keep it to yourself. **Be a Man.**

The Handyman: Home Repairs

Over the years, I've lived in a ton of different houses, condos, apartments, a couple of cars, and one ice-fishing shack. In each new home, I've attempted all types of home improvement projects. Some were great successes. A couple of them, yeah, they went the other way.

Start a new project every day and never finish any of them. **Be a Man.**

After getting married, I decided I was going to oversee the building of our new house. In most cases, people hire a general contractor to hire all the subcontractors and manage the job. Using a general contractor is a more expensive option but it usually takes a lot of headaches and stress out of the process. So I made sure I didn't do that.

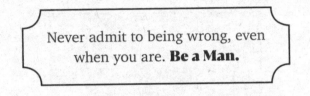

Never admit to being wrong, even when you are. **Be a Man.**

I interviewed and then hired framers, plumbers, HVAC engineers, electricians, and finish carpenters. Then I scheduled all the trades to start and finish work on schedule. One thing that most people don't understand until they have done it is the trickle-down effect on a construction job. When one thing goes wrong, it fouls up the whole job. Say the carpenters fail to secure a permit on time. Now instead of starting on a Friday, they can't start till Monday. The electricians were supposed to come on Monday but now they need to move it back, but the rest of their week is already booked on another job so now they are pushed into next week. And that trickle-down effect, that's not like a couple of drops of water dripping off your gutter. No, that's a little bit of snow trickling down from the top of a mountain. It picks up a little more snow and then a little more snow until it kicks off a massive avalanche of delays. One little scheduling delay and a project that should take three months can quickly turn into a five-month nightmare.

If you have to ask for help, don't! **Be a Man.**

We broke ground in May and started pouring the foundation. We got a slow start but the place was completely framed after a month. We were off and running. I was gonna save a ton of money and it was going to make me look like a hero to my wife. But after a few hiccups, our timelines started to get all screwed up. Shipments of items for the kitchen and the bathrooms were being delivered before the roof was even shingled. If you are a general contractor who does this every day, I'm sure you could have handled it much differently. But I was working during the day and running back and forth to the house to check in on the subcontractors and yeah, maybe there were a few details I may have missed. I was completely stressed out. After only a few weeks, I had already threatened the cabinet guy, the electrician, the foundation guys, and the guy delivering lumber.

> Never learn from your mistakes. **Be a Man.**

Listening to the radio on my way back from the city, I heard there was a big pop-up thunderstorm that was coming in around five o'clock that evening. If I didn't want my cabinets and appliances to get soaked, I needed to try and get a tarp on the roof. When you have a general contractor, this would normally be their job and their responsibility. But when I'm trying to act like a big shot and trying to run the show even though I have no idea what I'm doing, this lands directly on my shoulders.

I'm not sure if you have ever tried putting a sixty-foot tarp on the top of a house before, but it's not the most ideal situation, especially by yourself. I screwed the tarp down with strapping on one side as the winds started to pick up. My goal was to hold the other end of the tarp and walk up to the peak and down the other side to secure it. I didn't realize it at the time, but by trying to protect my stuff from the storm, I was assembling a massive wind-powered game of crack-the-whip.

When I was about halfway down the other side, a huge gust of wind got under the tarp and shot me fifteen feet in the air. I was still holding on to the tarp as I floated in the sky above the house. Nice little place shaping up below me, though it could definitely use more shingles. Right on cue, the sky opened up and it started to pour. The pressure pushed the tarp down and it whipped me, full speed, toward the roof. I slammed down like I was a bag of concrete and broke two ribs. As I gasped for breath, I continued to try and secure the tarp. After being thrown around like a rag doll for ten minutes, my side a white-hot inferno of pain, I was able to tie it down on the other side. So yeah, my Kenmore dishwasher didn't get wet but now my ribs hurt every time another storm is coming.

> If there is a tornado, don't go to the basement. Stand on the roof. **Be a Man.**

By the time we finished that job, I had put so much blood, sweat, pain, and suffering into it that I swore to my wife that we would grow old and die in that house. On cue a few years later, I decided we needed to move to another house further up north. The new house was in a decent neighborhood but it needed some work. It had three bathrooms and two of them were in good shape but the downstairs one really needed to be remodeled. The grout was cracking, the tiles were popping, and the whole thing smelled like an inch of water in an old rowboat. After living for years with my wife and two kids, I knew we needed three bathrooms fully operable at all times.

> If your wife wants to go to the beach on Saturday, start renovating your bathroom before she wakes up so you can't go. **Be a Man.**

Performing the necessary renovation would have to be done like a military operation—planning down to every last little detail, then flawless execution. So one night on a whim after drinking a few beers, I demoed the first-floor bathroom down to the studs. My wife freaked out. No problem, I told her, I knew a tile guy and a plumber who owed me favors, I'd get them in here, pop a new toilet and vanity in, and we'd have it buttoned up in two long days, three tops. But then my wife had a thing with her car that we had to take care of first. And then the tile guy disappeared on me. Between work, school stuff for the kids, and then their games after school, life started getting crazy. That bathroom stayed ripped apart for the next eight years.

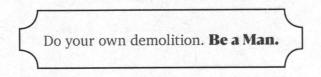

> Do your own demolition. **Be a Man.**

I finally made my brother, who is a contractor, come over and help me. We banged it out in a couple of weekends using a bunch of material he had left over from jobs. When it was all said and done, that bathroom had six different types of tile in it.

> While you're fixing the tiny leak under your sink, break three new things. **Be a Man.**

Of course, my wife (now ex-wife) was not happy with this. I was fine with it. I loved hanging with my crazy brother and making a bathroom with black and yellow tiles that looked like an ode to the Boston Bruins. The kids never wanted to use it, so it became my personal bathroom.

When we eventually split up, we sold the house. It went to some people who loved the place, and we did OK on it and made a little money. But most importantly, my bathroom was their favorite room in the house.

FIVE RENOVATION TIPS I'VE LEARNED

1. Always renovate the areas that need it most first.

2. Make sure functionality is a top priority.

3. Do your research and create a realistic budget.

4. Hire the right people and weigh the cost of hiring a professional.

5. Eh, fuck it, I'm just going to wing it, how hard can it be?

Our Happy Place

Nothing brings relief, satisfaction, and sometimes pure joy to a man quite like taking a good old-fashioned dump. There is just something about dropping ballast and disposing of unwanted cargo that clears the mind and refreshes the spirit. This daily ritual provides us with fifteen minutes (or more) of peace, quiet, and reflection. If there is one holy room in a man's castle—a sanctuary where he can take shelter from the noise of everyday existence and meditate on his life—it is the crapper.

Only use one-ply toilet paper. **Be a Man.**

The shitter is where we retreat to get away from our wife, our girlfriend, our kids, or our roommates. These days, bathrooms come in all shapes and sizes. They have full, half, and three-quarter layouts, each providing variations of styles and amenities. No matter if yours is as big as a ballroom with a chandelier and a fancy bidet to spritz your butthole with Perrier or it's a tiny mildewy closet so tight that your knees press up against the tub when you're dropping a bomb, that comforting feeling of seclusion remains.

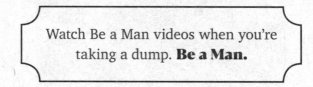

Watch Be a Man videos when you're taking a dump. **Be a Man.**

The home-court advantage is never greater than in the game of dropping a deuce. But sometimes the ultimate experience isn't available. When you hear that knock at your back door, you have to start making hard decisions. The idea of an unplanned operation in foreign territory—popping a squat in an unknown, uncharted public bathroom—is terrifying to some. But when you need to go, you need to go. It's never a good health decision to be the guy that holds it in. You don't ever want the best-case scenario to be that you nearly shit your pants.

Always trust a fart; shit your pants. **Be a Man.**

The modern marvel of indoor plumbing may be mankind's greatest accomplishment but sometimes we don't have the luxury of holding out for the peaceful, tiled comfort of an indoor facility. This can lead a desperate man to grab a heavy-duty contractor bag and yell for everyone in the vicinity to avert their eyes in order to steer clear of a traumatic incident, possibly one with civilian casualties.

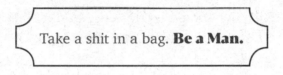

Take a shit in a bag. **Be a Man.**

When nature calls, don't be shy about taking a quick hobble out into the woods. There is nothing more freeing than giving back to nature and releasing compost back into the soil. Just drop trou, let the wind blow, and let one go. If you have never done this, you have never really lived.

Take a dump in the woods and wipe your ass with a pinecone. **Be a Man.**

One time in my mid-twenties, I was driving home from work right through Lynnfield into Lynn on Route 129 during rush hour. Suddenly, a powerful urge to purge came over me. I knew I was only ten minutes from home but I didn't have that kind of time. As the sweat poured down my face, I started to lose layers as fast as I could. I was clutching the steering wheel as I was hugging the turns like it was the only thing keeping my asshole closed. Just then a huge stomach gurgle rumbled through the car, drowning out the music on the radio. I couldn't wait another second. I pulled the car over to the side of the road, yanked the door open, and sprinted out right onto someone's front lawn. I squatted down like a dog just as all hell broke loose. I sat there as the traffic flew by with everyone staring at me, feeling nothing but satisfaction. Maybe even a little pride. There is no such thing as embarrassment when you really got to go.

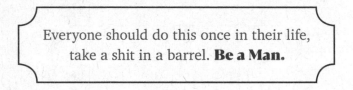

Everyone should do this once in their life, take a shit in a barrel. **Be a Man.**

Some people are totally against the idea of pulling the car over and running into the woods off the highway or squatting behind the dumpster at a CVS Pharmacy. For those delicate people, the next best option is using a clean public restroom. If you have the strength to hold it long enough, try and get to a department store or a Chick-fil-A. These are some of your best indoor options. The bottom-of-the-barrel choices are gas station lavatories and porta potties. When you consider these options, going in a regular public restroom or behind a bush doesn't seem that bad. Sometimes in life, you just need to face your fears headfirst. Or ass first.

If you're using a public bathroom, take a shit with the door open. **Be a Man.**

After experiences like these, any reservations you may have about using an unfamiliar public restroom will quickly melt away when you sit down on that crusty toilet seat and feel that first wave of sweet relief. Take a minute to enjoy it—this is probably the best you will feel in your entire life. Now shove that swinging door open, smile at a stranger, and own the moment.

FIVE BEST PLACES TO TAKE A DUMP

1. **YOUR OFFICE.** This is a home away from home. You know the territory and the layout, but picking your spot is also about picking your time, choosing the best opportunity. If you're not expecting visitors, hell yeah, hit the head closest to your office and enjoy the comfort and security. But if Janice in human resources down the hall runs out to Dunkin' in the middle of the morning, seize that opportunity to drop a coil in her personal bathroom so foul that it will ruin her day.

2. **HIGH-END HOTEL.** The biggest upside of a fancy hotel shitter is the cleanliness. They would never allow an overflowed toilet or a mess on the wall. These places have a full staff on the clock 24–7 to make sure this experience is seamless. They also possess only the finest amenities. Treat yourself to a double wipe with some triple-ply, maybe even throw a roll

or two in your jacket and bring some home to the wife.

3. **YOUR PARENTS' SECOND FLOOR HALF BATH.** Everyone knows this bathroom—the one your parents added later so your mom wouldn't have to share a bathroom with your dad. Another name for this bathroom is "The Reason Your Parents Aren't Divorced." It's the size of a broom closet because it's basically just a toilet, a little quarantine cube for your father to be alone with his stench. The fact that hardly anyone actually uses this bathroom gives it a unique feeling of comfort.

4. **THE WOODS.** Once you master them, the woods are the largest, most spacious bathroom in the world. Dumping in the woods is carefree, luxurious, but also somehow primal . . . this is the experience God intended when he created man's ability to pinch a loaf. Relax, spread out, enjoy yourself.

5. **THE OCEAN.** This one is underrated. Quick, easy, and undetectable. Now swim away fast.

Marriage: A New Beginning... of the End

In June 1992, my stress levels were at an all-time high. I was running books around the city on my own, my partying days were slowing down to a crawl, and in the middle of the month, I was getting fucking married.

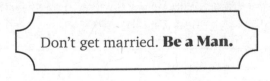

Don't get married. **Be a Man.**

In the weeks leading up to the ceremony, every single thing I needed to go right started to go wrong. My mom and dad had split years earlier and both of them were driving me nuts. They both wanted to know detailed lists of whom the other one was bringing. My mom had a new boyfriend and she was refusing to come if he wasn't invited while my dad was threatening that he and his friends weren't coming if my mom's boyfriend was there. It wasn't until four days before the ceremony that my dad committed to coming. He stopped by my house and grabbed twenty invitations to hand deliver to friends and family.

Get mad at your ex-wife and take it out on your kids. **Be a Man.**

Two days before we were set to walk down the aisle, the priest that was supposed to marry us kicked the bucket. Some might see this as a sign. I mean, is there a worse omen for a marriage than the priest dying before the ceremony? It sounds like an old Italian curse—God wanted us to not get married so badly that he was willing to kill a priest, one of his own, just to prevent it from happening. Of course, I ignored every warning and kept on trucking.

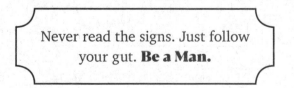

Never read the signs. Just follow your gut. **Be a Man.**

On the morning of the wedding, I woke up at the crack of dawn. I walked down to Fisherman's Beach with my brothers and we polished off a couple of cases of Bud, as we contemplated the day. Never a good combination. What the fuck was I about to do? Marriage was forever, you didn't just get a divorce in my family. I mean, my mom and dad did, but fuck them. I couldn't shake this bad feeling, like I was sailing into a storm. I decided it was just nerves about the wedding, that I just needed a couple of drinks to relax. Yeah, that's it, genius. I was about to join my life together in front of the law and God with a woman whom I already butted heads with daily, and it's the ceremony I was scared of. As long as I made it through the party, then we'd get to the good stuff: a mortgage, fighting in the car, long silent dinners, popping out a couple of kids, and then a sexless existence.

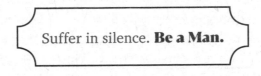

Suffer in silence. **Be a Man.**

It was the hottest day of the year. It was muggy, overcast, and misty. We pre-gamed at my brother's house, taking shots of sambuca to get ready for the long day. Then we were off to the church. There was no air conditioning at the church and when we walked in, the place was already like a sauna, everyone just sweating their balls off. At this point, I was already completely in the bag. I was ready to get this thing over with.

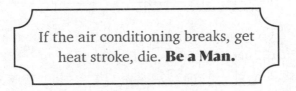

If the air conditioning breaks, get heat stroke, die. **Be a Man.**

After the ceremony, we got everyone loaded into the limo to head over to the reception. Once the last person had finally got in and slammed the door, right on cue, the driver backed over the curb and bottomed out the limo. It sounded like he ripped the entire undercarriage right off the vehicle. We drove about five minutes down the road before the limo was making so much noise and smoking so badly that we couldn't go any further.

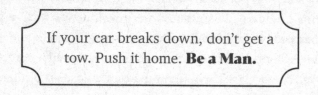

If your car breaks down, don't get a tow. Push it home. **Be a Man.**

So there we were, drenched in sweat on the side of the road, the whole wedding party trying to hitchhike. I'm in a full tuxedo and tails, this thick white collar suffocating me. My new wife is in a white dress with a twenty-foot train. This was long before cell phones and Uber; there was no way to call and no one to call if we could. We caught a ride in the back of a pickup like a bunch of hillbillies and showed up thirty minutes late to our own reception. By this point in the day, I was drunk, hot, and extremely frustrated. One more little shitty thing, and I was ready to explode.

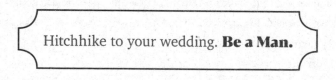

Hitchhike to your wedding. **Be a Man.**

The reception was held in one of those places that has waterfalls, wooden benches, and tons of ferns in the lobby. This place had multiple rooms so that you could have a bunch of weddings going at the same time. I was adamant about being the only party that day so we could have our privacy. The company assured us that the parties were on separate floors and that it wouldn't be an issue.

Finally, after all the bullshit, the party was just starting to get in a groove. Everyone had gotten their drinks and the waiters were making their rounds and serving dinner. Just then, the main dining room door swung open and slammed hard against the wall, getting everyone's attention. In marches a drunken conga line of at least thirty people from another fucking wedding. They went directly through the middle of the dance floor and around the tables like they owned the place. I couldn't believe what I was seeing. I was fuming and started to shake. My first reaction was *I'm going to kill these people.*

Get mad at everything instantly. **Be a Man.**

My brothers saw what was happening and immediately restrained me. I sat down and they momentarily released me. I discreetly slid two steak knives up my sleeves and made a run for the door. I was going to murder this other family. The entire wedding party got up to chase after me.

My new brother-in-law tried to stop me at the door.

"Don't do this, it's not worth it," he said.

"Get out of my fucking way!" I told him. When he refused, I ripped a clump of his hair out of his head and I was on my way.

I felt possessed. I don't know if it was the booze, the disrespect of the other wedding party, or the fact that I had just gotten married was sinking in. I ran downstairs, busted through the door to the other wedding, and tackled the guy leading the conga line. My momentum plowed us into a ten-foot-high champagne flute pyramid, smashing all of the glasses on the floor. It was a scene.

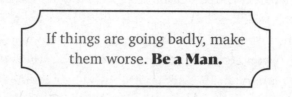

If things are going badly, make them worse. **Be a Man.**

The cops came and I was rushed out of a side door by my friends, now a fugitive on my own wedding day. By now, it was pouring outside and, as I walked down the street, I was quickly soaked to the bone. I started to sober up as everything started to come back into focus. *Holy shit*, I thought to myself, *I'm fucking married.*

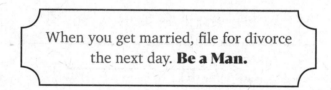

When you get married, file for divorce the next day. **Be a Man.**

The next morning, I got some encouraging words from my rough-around-the-edges dad. "Son," he said, "what a great fucking wedding!" One thing was for sure, it was one that no one there would ever forget. Who wants to go to a wedding, do some slow dances, and cut the cake, then stand around with a bunch of old people? Our wedding was like an episode of wrestling's *Saturday Night's Main Event*.

There is really no coming back from a wedding like that.

Don't watch your wife cry. Leave the room. **Be a Man.**

Hot and Cold

For one reason or another, men always dress the opposite of the season. When it's ten degrees outside, we throw on a pair of shorts to shovel in a blizzard. When it's a heatwave, we wear long pants to work. We are on a constant mission to prove to ourselves that we can handle whatever mother nature throws at us.

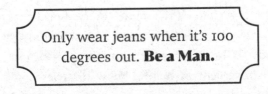

Only wear jeans when it's 100 degrees out. **Be a Man.**

When I was younger, I lived in a house with some buddies and we were all broke. We all had full-time jobs and were making money but our extracurricular expenses always seemed to outweigh our weekly paychecks. We had five guys living in a huge place with five bedrooms. You would think that with all those people, you could at least keep the utility bills paid. But by the time winter hit, we didn't have any money to get the oil tank filled. So we stocked up on blankets and jackets and hung them over the doorways. By February, all five of us were sleeping in the living room with one space heater.

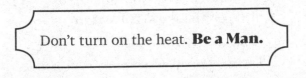

Don't turn on the heat. **Be a Man.**

In those early days, things weren't much different in the summer. Most places I lived just didn't have air conditioning. If we were lucky enough to live in a place equipped with air conditioning units, something always happened to break them and we were shit out of luck. Air conditioning was expensive enough but repairing a unit or buying new ones was a totally different ballgame. I'd rather perish.

> Don't get the air conditioning fixed. Just buy ten fans that don't do shit and sweat your ass off all summer long. **Be a Man.**

No matter if we had all the money in the world or we were dead broke, it was always instilled in us to never overindulge on useless material items. If we didn't need something, we didn't get it. No matter how convenient or helpful these luxuries could be in our everyday lives, it didn't matter. If you could live without it, you lived without it. More money for beer that way.

Winters in Massachusetts can get pretty brutal. Oftentimes, they seem like they will never end. People will suggest things to help alleviate the harsh cold, like hand warmers, winter hats, heated blankets, rum, and brandy. All of these options only create a temporary fix to a much bigger problem. Once you give in and start to get soft, there is no turning back.

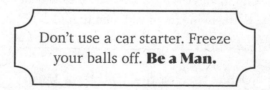

> Don't use a car starter. Freeze your balls off. **Be a Man.**

Don't use ChapStick. Let your lips scab up and bleed. **Be a Man.**

FIVE THINGS YOU DON'T NEED

1. **A WARM WINTER COAT.** Your father used this old peacoat and his father before him— what makes you special that you need a North Face instead of a fifty-year-old rag?

2. **POWER STEERING.** You drive the way a man drives—in constant pain.

3. **A HAIRCUT.** If it gets long enough to reach your mouth, just bite it off. This works for beards and mustaches too. If you can't see, cut the hair out of your eyes with toenail clippers.

4. **TV.** Use your imagination. Just sit back, close your eyes, and imagine yourself crawling into your neighbor's window and stealing their TV.

5. **FOOD.** Eat ice cubes—they're basically food.

Neighbors

Many people dream of hitting the lottery so they can live large, not a care in the world. The odds of this ever happening for you are about 1 in 250 million. The next greatest lottery you can hit has only slightly better odds but will probably have a greater impact on your life: having good neighbors. This can make the difference between loving your neighborhood and staying there for decades or moving out like a criminal in the middle of the night as soon as humanly possible. There are nosy, pitiful losers out there who have nothing better to do in this world than make your life a living hell. If you wind up with these types of neighbors, make it your life's mission to return the favor.

Take a dump on your neighbor's lawn
and say it was the dog. **Be a Man.**

Sometimes, you really hit the jackpot. You have a family move in next door where your kids are the same age, you drink the same kind of beer, and you both like hockey. When this happens, it's a gift from God. But in most cases, we find ourselves surrounded by petty, miserable pricks who can't stand anything about you. They will do whatever is in their power to take you down. These people yell at their kids, steal your newspaper and deny it, then call the cops if you're having some friends over.

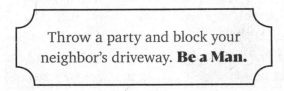

Throw a party and block your
neighbor's driveway. **Be a Man.**

When you have good neighbors, you take care of each other by doing neighborly gestures. You bring in their trash can if you're already taking in yours, you blow a path in the snow so they can get out during a blizzard. You lend them your SKIL saw if they are building a deck, give them a beer if it's getting hot outside, hell, maybe you even lend them a hand.

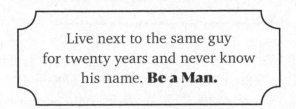

Live next to the same guy
for twenty years and never know
his name. **Be a Man.**

But when it comes to power tools and lending them out, it can be a slippery slope. Once a certain trust has been formed, your neighbors have no problem asking to borrow a tool or a ladder for the afternoon. Most times this isn't an issue. They finish the job and bring it right back.

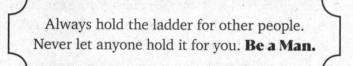

> Always hold the ladder for other people.
> Never let anyone hold it for you. **Be a Man.**

Other times, lending a tool can be the end of a once thriving relationship. This transaction can destroy an excellent working friendship in two different ways. Number one: they never return it. I don't care if it's a lug wrench I found on the side of the road. If I see you out in your backyard working on your lawn two weeks after you borrowed a tool from me and you smile in my face but don't say anything about it, you're dead to me. Number two (this may actually be worse than number one): when a neighbor borrows something, damages it, then returns it without offering to get you a new one or at least fix it. These people are truly the scum of the earth.

> If Jesus Christ himself moves in next
> door and asks if he can borrow a power
> tool, tell him no. **Be a Man.**

When I was twelve years old, we moved out of the city and into the suburbs twenty-five minutes north. For the first time in my life,

I felt out of place. The first day we moved in, our new next-door neighbor, an older lady with only one arm, brought us a hot apple pie to welcome us into the neighborhood. It felt like we were in a different world. We had never seen anything like it.

> Be nice to everyone . . . at first. **Be a Man.**

For the first little while, everything was great. But as time went on, our new friend next door with the one arm quickly turned from a friend to an enemy. Any time a ball went in her yard, she kept it, then destroyed it. If we were having fun and playing hockey in the driveway, she'd call the police and tell them we had explosives in the garage. The cops started making daily trips to our house as the calls just kept pouring in.

> Never call the cops on anyone for anything.
> Handle it yourself. **Be a Man.**

Being little kids at the time, there was only one way to get back at her without doing anything too crazy. Back in those days, you only had one phone. It was in the kitchen and there were no answering machines so when it rang, you picked it up. Every afternoon, this one-armed witch would tuck the newspaper under her arm, get her tea, then walk through the house and onto the front porch to read. As she only had one arm, it was a process for her to sit down and get situated. As soon as she had the paper opened on her lap, we would call her house. As the ring vibrated through the house and out onto the porch, she would carefully put her paper down, struggle to get up, then walk back inside through the front door. From our house, we would watch her walk through the house and toward the kitchen while we hid just below our window. When she was about a foot away and started to reach for the phone, we would hang up. We tallied up every time she called the cops or stole a ball and we made sure to make three times that many prank calls, till we were even.

Revenge is a dish best served daily. **Be a Man.**

Man's Best Friend

They say the best years of our lives are from fifteen to thirty years old. You've got no cares in the world, a new broad every few months, and a million friends to laugh and party with. We make big plans. We're gonna open a bar, we're gonna start a nightclub, we're gonna buy lake lots next to each other so we can bust balls when we're old men. These friendships are so powerful that you feel like these people will be with you for the rest of your life.

> If someone you're close to hates someone, you should hate them too. **Be a Man.**

When it comes to true friendship, it's all about trust. Knowing that your friends have your back 100 percent is one of the central requirements of a strong relationship. If your buddy has something important to tell you, no matter the significance, it's your job to guard that with respect and the utmost confidentiality.

> They say what happens in Vegas, stays in Vegas. How about this? Keep your fucking mouth shut all the time. **Be a Man.**

But as the years go by, people peel off one by one. The guy who was your best friend growing up ends up going down a different path, marries a religious Goody Two-shoes, becomes a man of God, and pretends he never smoked weed behind the dumpster at Arby's. Your college friends all move back home and you never see each other anymore. A deal with your first business partner goes sour and your friendship ends in bitterness.

> Never forgive anyone for anything, even when you can't remember what pissed you off. **Be a Man.**

People do normal stuff like get jobs and get married and have kids or they move away or maybe they go off the rails and go to prison. Some of them will even get sober and start selling Herbalife. We get busy chasing the shit we think is important—a boat, a pool, a timeshare in Colorado, a 401(k), braces for the kids, Xanax for the dog—while the stuff that's actually important slips away. Whatever the reason, friend by friend, people drop off to pursue their boring little adult lives, and your circle gets smaller and smaller.

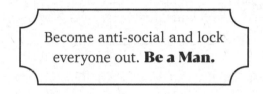

Become anti-social and lock everyone out. **Be a Man.**

You'll find you're guilty of it too. You have to bail on your regular Tuesday night happy hour with the boys because you have to pick the kids up from lacrosse practice. And you've already been sidelined from the hockey games for a while as you blew your ACL out years ago. You finally miss your annual boys' long weekend rager in Vegas as the goddamn dog your ex-wife made you get for the kids that they never walked or cleaned up after has too much anxiety to stay in the kennel. Congrats, dumbass, this is the rest of your life—an ex-wife who hates you, two kids who ignore you despite the iPhones that you paid for, and a neurotic German shepherd with dandruff and runny shits that you never wanted in the first place as your only company.

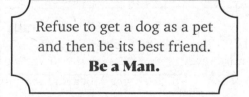

Refuse to get a dog as a pet and then be its best friend. **Be a Man.**

Yeah, as the years have gone by, your social circle has gotten so small that the dog she forced you to get is now the only true confidant you have. It's pathetic. You're pathetic. But it could be worse: you could have to rely on human beings for companionship.

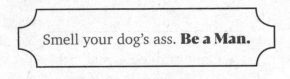

Smell your dog's ass. **Be a Man.**

In life we usually fear what we don't understand. To think that a German shepherd could be closer to you than all the guys you partied with in your twenties seems crazy. But these animals are always there and they always have your back, even when they don't want to. The dog is not about to grow thumbs and steal your car and bail on you. It's so neurotic anyway that it's not like someone is going to steal it. And that dog will keep your secrets. If your girlfriend asks the dog if you went to a titty bar when you said you had a friend's memorial, it's not gonna rat you out. It's not even going to stammer through a dumb lie. It's not gonna say one word, it's gonna keep its mouth shut and carry your secrets to the grave. If you had to choose the dog or an inseparable friend from twenty years ago the answer is clear. The dog wins, every time.

When your dog's taking a shit, take one next to him. **Be a Man.**

FIVE REASONS WHY YOUR DOG IS BETTER THAN YOUR FRIENDS

1. **SUPERIOR PERSONALITY.** They say that dogs' personalities are a direct result of how the people who own them treat them. Since I treat my dogs better than I treat any person I know, the choice is easy.

2. **THEY NEVER HOLD A GRUDGE.** Sure, they might be mad at you when you leave them all day while you were out. But they don't hold anything against you. As soon as you walk in the door, their bad energy instantly disappears and it's all water under the bridge.

3. **KEEPING US ACTIVE.** If your buddy asks you to throw the ball around, you tell him to piss off. But when the dog chews on your slipper and cries at the door to go for a run, you jump to it because you don't want them to shit on the floor. They have successfully found a way to get you off the couch and out of the house.

4. **HELP MOVING.** The worst friend of all is the one that calls you to help them move. This is something that your dog will never do.

5. **NEVER UNFAITHFUL.** Your dog may snuggle up to your girlfriend on the couch or in the bed but they will never try to bang your girlfriend. Well, they never succeed, anyway.

Grass-Fed, Free-Range Masculinity

> If there's a tsunami, go down to the beach. **Be a Man.**

Over the past couple of years, I have been asked a ton of times about the phrase "toxic masculinity" and what it means to me. I think in this world, most things can be understood differently once we've seen them through someone else's eyes. Masculinity can mean different things to different people and that's OK.

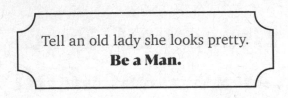

Tell an old lady she looks pretty.
Be a Man.

When I was growing up, masculinity meant not showing emotions and standing strong no matter what the situation. To some people, showing vulnerability and opening up is part of growing as a man. We can talk till we're blue in the face about what makes a man and not get anywhere but one thing's for certain: if you don't define for yourself what makes a man, there's no way you can meet those goals. If you don't care about what it means to be a man enough to spell it out to yourself, you will never be a man. No matter how we see manliness and masculinity, it's up to us to own it.

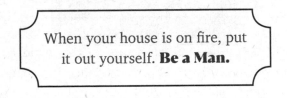

When your house is on fire, put
it out yourself. **Be a Man.**

The way I was raised, if you have a problem, you deal with it. Too many times in life, people don't deal with their problems, they let them escalate until they're impossible to control. My dad used to say, "Unfinished business is like a dark cloud floating over your head." Growing up with two brothers, I always knew someone had my back. But we also knew first and foremost that you had to rely on yourself. If you got knocked down, your brother would be there to help you get back on your feet, but he wasn't always going to get knocked down for you.

> Fuck all the small talk. Get to the
> fucking point. **Be a Man.**

Over the last ten years, society has tried to tell men that it's not OK to act like men. We're told we can't be competitive, we can't be self-reliant, we can't take risks. If you don't want to compete or you're content with sitting on the sidelines, that's your choice. For some of us, though, these are the attributes that make us feel alive. These attributes are the exact reasons why we're able to have the strength to take chances and to pull off our greatest accomplishments.

> Tell your kids that winning is
> everything. **Be a Man.**

Some of the most significant men in the world have persevered and achieved greatness because of their confidence in their own abilities. Instead of telling people it's unhealthy to want to be a leader or a protector, maybe we should be teaching more kids how to build confidence so they can do whatever they want to do while also protecting the people around them. You hear people say masculinity is toxic as if it was always an invitation to commit violence when in reality it's always been a way to protect yourself against it.

> Beat up a bully. **Be a Man.**

For centuries, it's been working class men who have kept the world moving. They fix your toilets, they fix your cars, they build your houses, they dig the trenches and run the power lines so you can turn on the lights to read this book or eat your dinner or do pretty much anything you do. Sometimes these men are considered toxic because they are rough around the edges and say what's on their minds but these men are oftentimes honest, hardworking, manly, and essential. These are hard jobs, and sometimes a hard job requires a rough touch. If you're thankful for the products of those hard jobs—running water, electricity, highways, gasoline—be thankful for the manly men who make them happen for you. If these men seem primitive to you, you should understand that the refined modern world would crumble without them.

> Power go out? Climb the pole
> yourself and fix it. **Be a Man.**

You cannot make an omelet without breaking eggs. We've all heard that before. But if for some reason you can't bear to break those eggs, so instead you pay someone to break them for you, don't pretend it never happened. While you're enjoying your omelet, think of them with gratitude because it wouldn't have happened without them. The hard work of hard men is integral to our everyday lives, and they are owed a place at the table. It's not just OK to let men be men, it's essential.

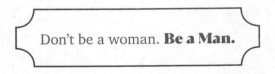

> Don't be a woman. **Be a Man.**

How to Satisfy Your Woman

They say a healthy relationship is all about communication. As a man, you should be attentive to all aspects of a woman's needs, both in and out of the bedroom. Women will tell you what they like, you just need to tune in. Women love to express themselves and share their feelings. We should never try to fix them or change them but rather love them for who they are. Sometimes they don't want advice but rather just the assurance that someone is there listening.

> Never listen. **Be a Man.**

She loves to be appreciated for the little things. She feels like we overlook what she does for the family and the house on a regular basis. It's in a woman's nature to nurture but their constant work to help others is many times ignored. From what they do for our children to how they empower us to make us better men, we take them for granted. Show her you're paying attention to these minuscule but oh-so-important details by checking in with her. Ask her frequently, "Are you gaining weight?" If she's having a tough day or dealing with loss or she's just getting really stressed out, show her you're on her side by saying, "Are you having your period?"

> If your girl cuts her hair or paints a room in the house, don't notice it. **Be a Man.**

She has pet peeves about a lot of the things you do on a daily basis. She just wants you to be conscious of these things and fix them. The best thing you can do for the relationship is to be the best version of yourself. She wants you to grow, learn, and work on self-improvement. Is it too much for her to ask you to change every single little thing about yourself? For example, she doesn't like how you act when you go out drinking with the boys. So maybe it's time to start inviting them over to drink at your house more often. She hates how you pick your nose at the dinner table, so next time use a Kleenex . . . then leave it on the table. By making helpful compromises like these, you'll quickly find that she has fewer things about you she wants to change.

> Don't fold clothes. Just roll them up in a ball and throw them in the drawer. **Be a Man.**

When we don't have much left to hold on to in the house, one thing men fight to keep control of is the TV remote. Men like watching documentaries about World War II and mafia crime syndicates or superhero movies with lots of boobs and explosions, or maybe a feel-good story about an alienated loner who turns his Caterpillar tractor into an armored tank and destroys his town. And we don't care who's next to us while we're watching. Your broad doesn't just want to watch some dusty old moth-eaten Victorian romance or that one movie where Heath Ledger is a knight who line dances, she wants to watch them with you. Show her how much you love her, how much she matters to you, how much you respect how much she contributes to your household by yielding the remote to her one night. Then spend the entire movie looking at your phone. If she objects, agree to put your phone down, then get up and go to the bathroom. When you return forty-five minutes later and she's weeping over some love scene, just plop down and say, "What'd I miss?"

> When your girl tells you to get
> in touch with your emotions, punch
> a hole in the wall. **Be a Man.**

Women love the idea of celebrating the anniversaries of special events in your life together. They drop hints in the weeks that lead up to the big date and even show you internet links to things they would love to get for a future present. "It doesn't have to be anything crazy," they say, as they show you expensive jewelry, cruises to Greece, and ridiculously overpriced yard furniture. Really, she just wants to be heard, to know that you recall all the special moments that represent the amazing journey you've had together. Showing her you remember is showing her you care. Try little things like, "Hey, remember sophomore year of college when you got so drunk that you slept under your car?" Take hints when they are offered to you: "Facebook says your dumb old cat died three years ago today." If you have kids together, be sure to bring them into the celebration: "Do you little shits remember that this time last year, your mother was getting dragged out of a Filene's Basement because of you?"

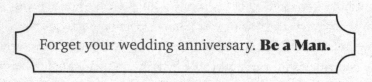

Forget your wedding anniversary. **Be a Man.**

Be a Dad

Expecting a child? Don't buy a minivan, buy a Vette. **Be a Man.**

Growing up around old school Italians, extracting information was like trying to pull blood from a stone. So when I had kids, I tended to adopt similar traits. They say communication is the key to great relationships, but I've done pretty well over the years barely expressing myself.

> If your wife's having a baby, don't hold her legs. Go to the bar and pick her up later. **Be a Man.**

My dad was a provider who protected his family and always led by example. When I got married and started a family, I was the same way with my kids. I made sure they always had food, clothing, and shelter, maybe even a bike and a couple of bucks in their pocket. I taught them right and wrong through my actions. I tried to pass down to them the wisdom that was passed down to me.

> Make your kid hold the flashlight and call it a lesson. **Be a Man.**

The age that I grew up in, when me or my brothers fucked up, we got "The Strap." Or maybe, if we were lucky, my dad would just smack us around with his humongous hands. My father had hands the size of baseball mitts. These days, it's considered abuse. But when I was a kid, that was just being disciplined on a Saturday night. When you got taught a lesson for being a punk, you didn't forget it and you did your best to not let it happen again. Kids are softer than ever these days. It's not necessarily their fault, a lot of that is directly handed down by how soft the parents have been on them. Nowadays, parents want to be their kids' best friends. My parents didn't care about any of that. They just wanted to raise good kids that were respectful.

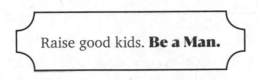

Raise good kids. **Be a Man.**

Growing up, life was simple. We didn't have a million rules to follow, but the ones we did have were written in stone. Be home by curfew, respect women by never laying a finger on them and always protecting them, and never leave the table until you've been excused. Every night after dinner, we would always have to ask to be excused. I would add some bass in my voice and say, "Dad, may I be excused?" Ninety percent of the time he wouldn't answer or look me in the eye. He would just stare straight ahead like he didn't hear anything. After a few moments of silence, I would clear my throat and try again.

"Excuse me, Dad, can I be excused?"

"Ask your mother," he'd grumble under his breath.

Families barely eat together these days, let alone eat in the dining room. In those days, we ate in the dining room, so by this point, my mother was already in the kitchen doing the dishes. I got up to walk into the other room to see my mother.

The minute I left the room, my father stood up and yelled, "Who told you you could leave the table?"

I ran back to my seat and sat down. I sat there in silence till he took his time finishing eating in slow motion. Only after he finished gnawing on the last bone, got up, and took his perch on the couch did he declare, "*Now* you may be excused."

The ball breaking was endless.

Back in those days, if we messed up any of these rules there were consequences to pay. When I became a dad, I adopted the same set of rules.

If someone messes with your kids, go to their parents' house and fight their father. **Be a Man.**

As dads, we all seem to like similar things. We love beer, sports, fires, cooking out on the grill, and driving around aimlessly alone. When we are in the living room after a long day we never like to sit down, we want to lie down on the couch. We insist that we need to watch a game or a show that we've been waiting for all day. Then before you know it, we're snoring. Another hard day of parenting is done.

Fall asleep watching TV, then get pissed off when somebody changes the channel. **Be a Man.**

Man Meets World

No two men are the same but somehow we all have the same favorite place: alone, inside our heads. Unfortunately, we occasionally have to venture out into the real world and interact with human beings. It's another unpleasant side effect of being alive. All places are bad, but some are less bad than others.

GOING TO THE HARDWARE STORE

We do everything in our power to stay out of stores. We are constantly nagged by the women in our lives, "Just go in for a minute, you'll like it." But we never like it, not once. The only store that we can go into on a regular basis and keep going back to is the hardware store. Doesn't matter if it's Lowe's, The Home Depot, Ace Hardware, or a tiny mom-and-pop outfit. As long as they have power tools, nuts and bolts, and lumber, I can spend any amount of time wandering around, looking at a bunch of shit I'll probably never buy and a couple of things I'll buy and never use. Special shout-out to Ace because you can walk in with a screw from 1914 and say, "I need eight of these except in brass," and they have an old guy who does just that.

TALKING TO THE MECHANIC

The mechanic is a different breed. Their entire existence is making a living by lying on the ground as oil drips in their face. They are rough around the edges and aren't necessarily known for their communication skills so make sure you are clear and on point with your instructions. Here are a few things to never say to a mechanic: "Do whatever it takes," or "I don't know the first thing about cars," or "Just call me when it's done." These phrases are a clear invitation to bend you over a barrel.

GOING FISHING

We are simple beings who can't do too many things at once. While women are excellent at multitasking, fishing is the perfect way for us to shut off our brains and just focus on one simple thing. There is no real thought process that goes into a day of fishing. We simply put some bait on the line and drop it in the water. Then we sit there for the next couple of hours, drinking beers and waiting for something to bite. This is the type of sport we can get behind. In an ideal situation, you will run out of beer and have to go home before you catch anything so you won't have to clean any disgusting fish. They have trout at the grocery store, just remember to unwrap it before you get home.

GOING HUNTING

Hunting and fishing are the two greatest connections we have to our ancestral roots. Men have always been hunter-gatherers whose main job was to collect food for the family. What makes hunting so important for men is that it reconnects us with our food. When we go to the store and buy a couple of steaks, we don't appreciate the struggle of what it took to eat that meal. There is no greater satisfaction than the pursuit and conquering of finding your next meal. After sitting in a deer blind for eight hours, bored out of your skull, you will have a new appreciation for all the work that went into the six pounds of beef jerky you ate.

HANGING AT YOUR LOCAL BAR

Everyone needs a favorite bar, the kind of place where everyone knows your name and the bartender already has your drink on the bar by the time you sit down. These places are vital to the community. Sure, it's nice to throw back a few beers and a couple dozen wings, get a little shine on, and escape your wife and children.

But the fact that you can shoot the shit with friends, support local businesses, and discover new local musicians is the real win. These places are an integral part of building a thriving community. Anyway, that's what you tell your wife when she says you're not allowed to go anymore.

GOING TO YOUR FAVORITE RESTAURANT

Some people love to go out and paint the town red, go on wild adventures, and enjoy a new restaurant every weekend. For us, once we find one that we like, that's it. We will literally go to the same spot every Friday night for the next twenty years, study every item on the menu, then order the same exact meal every time.

The In-Laws

From the time we are very little to when we are old and decrepit, dealing with our families is challenging at best. We find a way to move out of our parents' house as soon as possible and often alienate family members for years at a time. We can handle being around the entire family only a couple of times a year, on the holidays. Even then, it takes the sedation that comes with way too much food and tons of booze to prevent an all-out brawl.

> If you're sitting down for holiday dinner and someone starts talking politics, throw mashed potatoes at their head. **Be a Man.**

It takes a lot of work to find the right person to marry. You have to convince yourself that you have finally found that special one, despite your drunken screaming matches and backhanded sniping and other obvious red flags. Just when you've finally convinced yourself that you can live in mounting resentment with this person forever, a new family gets thrust into the picture. It was one thing to have to deal with your family that's related by blood—you were born into it. But now you need to be cordial to people you would never choose to be in the room with in a million years.

Need to get away from the family for the weekend? Fake a heart attack. **Be a Man.**

Your relationship with your new in-laws is an important one because it goes much deeper than how you personally get along with them. These people are connected to you in complicated ways as they are not only your wife's parents but also your kids' grandparents. If you talk shit about them to your wife, it will only make your life even more complex.

If your in-laws come over to the house, jump out the window. **Be a Man.**

Sometimes you get lucky and you get paired with a set of in-laws that are tolerable. You can talk about sports or food or cars, or you have similar hobbies. But the ones who draw a bad hand are in for the nightmare of dealing with passive aggressive, disrespectful, and miserable people for decades, maybe even the rest of your life. In a perfect world, we'd get along great with everyone. But with our in-laws, sometimes that just isn't possible.

Tell your mother-in-law to shut up. **Be a Man.**

FIVE WAYS TO AVOID YOUR IN-LAWS

1. **FAKE A MIGRAINE.** If you have ever had a migraine, you know how brutal these things can be. You feel like you are gonna puke, you can't see straight, and it completely derails your daily plans. Make sure to have all of your electronics charged and retreat to the bedroom to lie down in a dark room until it passes. Then play Play-Station all day with your headphones on and never return.

2. **START A HUGE PROJECT.** If you know your in-laws are coming over in the afternoon, make sure to start taking the engine apart on the hot rod a couple hours before they arrive. This way you will have the entire project in a thousand pieces spread across the driveway when they get there. Now you have no choice but to hammer away at it until you get it all back together. Maybe stash your beer in a cooler directly under the engine bay so that every time your curious brother-in-law comes out, you're under the hood.

3. **WORK EMERGENCY.** The first key is NEVER letting them fully understand what it is you actually do for work. Once that is established,

anything you make up can be a plausible emergency. "The servers are down, there was a chemical spill in the basement that shut down operations. I need to get over to the office right now to turn everything back on manually before we lose all the data." They don't need to know that you work the register at Lowe's Garden Center.

4. **GET A ROTTWEILER.** If your mother-in-law is deathly afraid of dogs, especially big scary ones, this is a solution that can quickly discontinue her voyages to the homestead.

5. **MOVE ACROSS THE COUNTRY.** People will come over to the house every day if they are "in the neighborhood." When your house is three thousand miles across the country, there is no such thing as a drop-in visit. Now they need to plan a trip, buy a plane ticket, and find someone to watch the animals at their house. Them coming over twice a week turns into once a year. Weird thing is that there's a chemical spill in the basement at your job just about once a year too.

Keep the Doctor Away

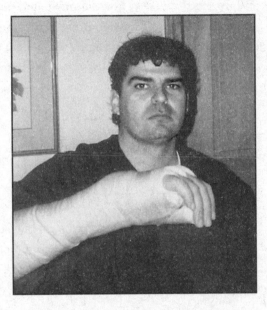

As men, it's our duty to remain extremely headstrong in moments of great pain. On top of that heroic burden, if the pain has been inflicted by our own stupidity, we must double down at all costs.

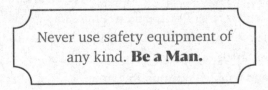

Never use safety equipment of any kind. **Be a Man.**

A couple years back, I was working on a shed in my backyard. I was using a nail gun with an air compressor and you'd be amazed at what a great tool that is for shooting a nail right through your foot. After taking off my shoe and sock, it was immediately clear that this wound was going to require professional medical attention, probably multiple stitches. So I dipped a rag in some alcohol from the basement and grabbed some electrical tape—a little electrical tape can heal anything.

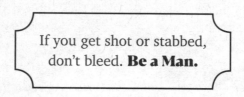

If you get shot or stabbed, don't bleed. **Be a Man.**

I've had tons of friends over the years who do blue-collar labor. As I've said, this type of work is usually underappreciated but is truly the backbone of our society. One thing these people all have in common is a strong hatred for medical facilities.

Don't file for disability. Work until your bones turn into powder. **Be a Man.**

There are many ways to ruin your own day, from losing fingers on a table saw to blowing out your back on a slip and fall to burning through several layers of skin on a hot manifold gasket. A friend of mine once fell thirty-seven feet off a ladder, landed on a picnic table, and broke his ankle. Ten days later, he was back on the job with his ribs taped and hobbling around in a boot.

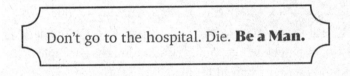

If you get hurt, don't make a sound. **Be a Man.**

Men avoid hospitals for many reasons. We don't like to be told we need to quit doing something we love like eating or drinking, and we don't like being told we need to be more careful. As men, we believe we should be strong enough to handle things on our own. More importantly, we know that we won't like hearing what they have to say anyways. When you work for yourself, hearing that you can't work is the worst news there is. The best way to not hear the bad news is to not listen. I've only been to a hospital a handful of times and every time I got there, it's because I was unconscious.

Don't go to the hospital. Die. **Be a Man.**

A few years back, I was playing in a softball game with my brother. Late in the game, I hit a bullet in the gap. Right out of the box, I was thinking two. I hustled to first and as soon as I hit the bag, I heard a pop and got a sharp pain in my foot. I thought someone shot me in the heel, I hit the dirt like a ton of bricks. I didn't twist my ankle at all so I didn't know what the hell happened but apparently I had torn my Achilles. Everyone came out to carry me off the field but I refused. It probably took twice as long but I made sure that I didn't get any help.

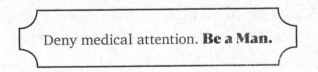

Deny medical attention. **Be a Man.**

The Man of Leisure

Men can be the hardest working, most relentless workaholics. When it comes to our jobs, our careers, and our dreams, we are unmovable. We refuse to take days off or go on vacations because there is work to be done and we won't stop till it's finished. We can focus on something and grind like maniacs till we achieve it. When we put the blinders on, everything around us falls by the wayside.

Work till you're dead, then stay a couple more hours because it's time and a half. **Be a Man.**

But if it's a Sunday, you have a few friends over for the game, and you're drinking beers, all bets are off. Men built this great country, but men can also be the most unproductive, laziest, most slothful pieces of shit in the world. We can immediately switch from tireless robotic machines into the world's greatest procrastinators. A rule of thumb is that if I'm standing up, there is nothing I can't do. But if I lie down on the couch for even one minute, don't expect me to do anything for the rest of the day.

Take up the entire couch. **Be a Man.**

A lot of times, men become workaholics as a way to separate themselves from people, feelings, and family. We prioritize work over everything and thrive off the excitement of doing the impossible. When you live like this, there is no break from work regardless of the situation.

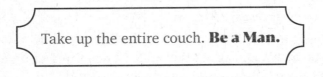

Don't work a nine-to-five.
Work 24–7. **Be a Man.**

The next rung down the ladder from workaholics is "hard workers." These are the people who get shit done but still find time for people close to them as well as for themselves. I've always wanted to relax and enjoy myself but I've always had a hard time doing it. We go on vacations and hop on the computer, we take business calls down by the pool and cut vacations short to get back to a pressing matter. Unlike workaholics, hard workers are able to find a balance between their personal lives and their work. I don't understand these people and, honestly, I hope I never do.

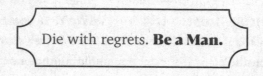

Die with regrets. **Be a Man.**

That said, as the years go by and I get older, the days of being a workaholic are disappearing in the rearview. My goal now is to try and enjoy some of the shit I never did, all the shit I never had time for. I still have a lot of good things ahead of me but it's time to free myself from any obligations to other people.

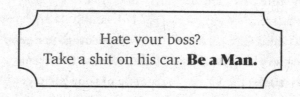

Hate your boss?
Take a shit on his car. **Be a Man.**

The ultimate goal with any man is to be a true man of leisure, someone who can make enough money to live comfortably while doing as little work as possible. I fucking hate these guys.

Retire, then go back to work two days later because you're sick of your family. **Be a Man.**

FIVE WAYS FOR MEN TO RELAX

1. **HOSE DOWN THE DRIVEWAY.** If you had a tough day at work, there is no better way to crank it down a notch than holding the hose for an hour as it sprays water all over the driveway. No, this won't do anything for the oil stains on the pavement from your 1986 C10, but that's not the point. You could easily use a blower and clear the pine needles, cat litter, and debris in seconds but this is more therapeutic than anything.

2. **GET A MASSAGE.** Getting a massage is a great way to release stress. The minute they remove their elbow from the middle of your back, you'll feel better.

3. **GRILL AND DRINK.** I can think of no better way to relax on a 100-degree day than by standing over a 600-degree grill with a cooler of endless ice-cold beers. You can feel the stress literally melt away.

4. **CLEAN THE CAR.** A lot of times, we take great pride in the cars that we drive. So when we take one out on the town or go out on a date we want

it to look top notch. Wash and wax the outside, detail the interior, run that hunka junk through a damn time machine if you can.

5. **WORK SIXTEEN-HOUR DAYS.** The best way to get away from the hardships of life is to just put your head down and work some more.

Going Against the Grain

In life, there have always been two roads to choose from. There's the one that most of the world tramples down and uses daily. Then there's the other, a less traveled path that holds the endless possibilities of "what if." It's easy to choose the road that's properly lit and paved. But it takes a certain kind of driven, unhinged person who chooses to drive through brush and rutted roads to get where you're going. I learned early on in life that going against the grain would always create more opportunities and experiences no matter how fucked up they might be.

Speed bumps? Fuck it. Floor it. **Be a Man.**

People always tell you to get a good job, work hard, and move up the ranks. After thirty years, you'll have a 401(k) and some savings that you can lean on as you start to slow down and become less productive. That's the plan, anyway. Even when I worked regular jobs, that was never my mindset. If you really wanna break ground and make a difference in anything in life, you need to be focused on it all the time and always grinding. You want to do something bad enough, you will work one job to pay the bills during the day and start moonlighting at night doing what you really want till it becomes a reality.

> Don't use the stairs. Scale the building. **Be a Man.**

When we do take time away from working, we like to have a few drinks to relax. We like to drink as a way to socialize, have a little fun, and forget about our lives for a minute. When the bills pile up and your girl is up your ass, going out for a drink with the boys is one of the most freeing feelings in the world. We can kick back and talk about sports and cars and forget about all of the daily bullshit. But you can't make kicking back your daily routine. Drinking is great until you wake up one day and it's not.

> If you're in an alcohol-induced coma, wake up and have a drink. **Be a Man.**

Morning Routine

I've been doing the same morning routine for the past thirty or forty years. The most important part of dominating the day is waking up early. My dad used to say, "If you wake up at 9:00 A.M., the day is already half over." I don't use alarm clocks either, I just mentally tell myself 4:00 A.M. is when I'm getting up and as soon as it hits, I spring out of bed like there's a fire alarm going off. When you're young, you think it's cool to stay up late and sleep all day. But as you grow up, you realize the boss shit is waking up early and getting shit done while everyone else is sleeping.

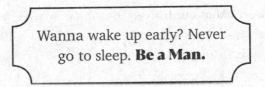

Wanna wake up early? Never go to sleep. **Be a Man.**

Some people need to get out of bed, eat breakfast, and drink water before hitting the bathroom. Not me. Every morning like clockwork, I beeline it from the bed directly to the toilet to drop off the morning refuse. Some people eat cereal, oatmeal, protein shakes, and toast. I make a nice pot of black coffee, throw the TV on with no sound, put on a podcast, and start shadow boxing. After I've worked up a little sweat, I get in the kitchen and cook a pound of bacon and half a dozen eggs to get the sustained energy I need.

Fry bacon with your shirt off. **Be a Man.**

FIVE MORNING RITUALS

1. Take an ice-cold shower.

2. Stare at the wall.

3. If your hands are dry, don't use lotion, spit on 'em.

4. Don't drink coffee, eat the beans.

5. Don't drink milk, breastfeed until you're seventy-five.

Lord of the Manor

The older we get, the less we actually enjoy anything. When we're young, we love playing sports, running after broads, going to concerts, and partying. After we've had our fun and the party is over, our perspective shifts. After all of our big dreams have been dashed, there are only a few things that actually bring happiness.

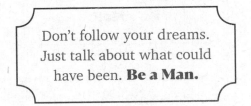

Don't follow your dreams. Just talk about what could have been. **Be a Man.**

We make decisions and plot our life's turns based on how much pleasure we will get out of them. How much pleasure we'll get and how much pain we will have to endure. When we were young, the ultimate was an action-packed weekend hanging with the boys in Vegas, drinking and gambling and chasing broads, getting kicked out of casinos and hotels, maybe even off-roading or skydiving or a bench-clearing brawl. Or maybe a big fishing trip up to the lake—a long hot drive and then beers and boating and a massive campfire, then sleeping out under the stars with the bugs and the bears.

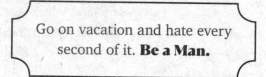

Go on vacation and hate every second of it. **Be a Man.**

But as we get older and more jaded, sitting on a chair in the backyard with a cold cocktail and looking at the lawn is about as good as it gets. We don't seek out the adventures like we once did, but we also don't pay the price. Now simplicity and silence are our greatest joys.

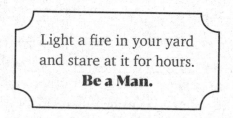

Light a fire in your yard and stare at it for hours. **Be a Man.**

Your home is the place you're supposed to be you, the place where you can forget about everything. It's comfortable, you got the cooler packed, you have the perfect chair to watch the game, and your clothes are scattered everywhere so they're easy to find.

> Hire a cleaning lady but don't let her touch anything. **Be a Man.**

The only thing that can change this incredible vibe is a new "roommate." Throughout life, these nightmares can come in the form of random slobs from college, old druggy friends, the friend getting a divorce you let crash for one night who has been on your couch for six months, psychotic girlfriends, bitter wives, and screaming children. Each of these bad options represents distinct attacks on your peace and quiet.

> If you're stuck with a roommate from hell, lock up your valuables and pretend they don't exist.
> **Be a Man.**

Being the man of the house no longer means you're king of the castle. These days, being the man of the house means that you have part of the basement and a corner of the yard on lock. The rest has been seized and controlled by the opposition. We don't fix things for the reasons you might think. We will work on a car in the driveway or fix the lawnmower in the yard just so we have something to do alone. Contrary to the official public narrative, men don't fix things because it's fun or fulfilling. We fix them because we might need a getaway car.

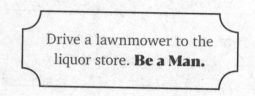

Drive a lawnmower to the
liquor store. **Be a Man.**

Most relationships in life are longer than they have to be. There are people we meet who we were supposed to meet and have crazy adventures and meaningful experiences that result in lifelong bonds. There are other people, too, people we never should have spent more than a few minutes with who end up hanging around for years. Dating is fine, even having friends is fine. But these people need to live off premises. Once they move in under the same roof, it's never the same.

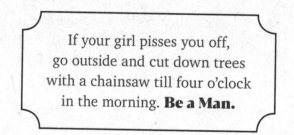

If your girl pisses you off,
go outside and cut down trees
with a chainsaw till four o'clock
in the morning. **Be a Man.**

FIVE THINGS THAT BELONG IN EVERY MAN'S HOUSE

1. Shitloads of power tools.

2. A basket of remote controls that don't go to anything.

3. A wad of cash in the freezer.

4. A *Penthouse* magazine from the '80s.

5. A car engine on a coffee table.

Live Free and Die

As men, we don't want to live unless we are living on our terms. We are accustomed to our freedoms; without them we are nothing. We tell our families that if we're ever in a bad accident and we can't walk or talk, to end it, but since when were you ever able to count on your family for anything?

Unplug your own life support. **Be a Man.**

Everyone is different but for the most part, men are street smart more than book smart. What we learn outside of school, in the real world, on the job, and from our peers just turns out to be more useful. We learn how to form questions to get the answers we need, we learn to rely on our common sense, and we learn how to sniff out bullshit from a mile away. In the process, we create logic that only we understand. No matter how ridiculous it might seem to others, we always do things our way

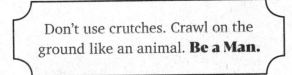

Don't use crutches. Crawl on the ground like an animal. **Be a Man.**

We were always told to go to college, get an education, and get a job that doesn't beat the shit out of our body. In many cases we suck at school, hate the idea of boring desk jobs, and somehow feel relieved settling back into the blue-collar workforce. Sure, maybe we make less money and the chances of getting hurt on the job are greatly increased. But we can't bear feeling like we are trapped in a cubicle, so we're happy to deal with all the shit that comes along with physical labor. These jobs can be treacherous—working on rooftops, in crawl spaces, on high-voltage power lines and around dangerous equipment. Sure, we might be miserable at times but when you live in fear of being maimed or killed, well, it isn't boring.

Don't go to college. Work on the factory floor of a steel mill until you die. **Be a Man.**

When it comes to safety on the job, in the car, or around the house, we don't really pay too much attention. When we get a new table saw, the first thing we do is take the guard off and throw it away. We don't wear helmets, we don't use harnesses on the roof, and we go to the dealership to have them remove the beep so we can drive around without the seat belt. Some might think we are just stupid animals who can't accept our mortality, but we would honestly rather die than be restricted.

> Don't use airbags. Fly through the window. **Be a Man.**

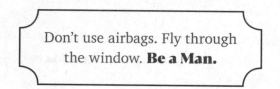

FIVE INJURIES EVERY MAN NEEDS

1. **DOUBLE HERNIA.** Don't get it fixed, why would you? Make your kids squeal by popping your guts in and out.

2. **LOSE A FINGER.** God didn't give you ten because you need all of them. Six of those are spares—you can drink, smoke, and drive with lobster claws. He who dies with the most fingers loses.

3. **SHRAPNEL IN YOUR BODY.** Don't get it removed so you set off every metal detector you go through and inconvenience your entire family when you're flying somewhere on vacation.

4. **PARTIAL DENTURE.** Never clean it. Spit out that filthy, tobacco-stained abomination to scare children or every time you laugh.

5. **AT LEAST ONE MAJOR BROKEN BONE.** How else are you going to know when it's about to rain?

Be a Caveman

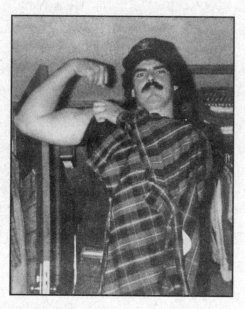

Nearly 200,000 years ago, the first Neanderthals roamed the earth. They lived in dark caves, made tools from stone, and were the first humanoids to adapt by cooking meat over a fire. Although we have evolved over thousands and thousands of years from our ape-like ancestors, there are many things that still have never changed. We may have developed physically and emotionally but we remain knuckle-draggers at our core.

> Don't use electronics on the plane.
> Just stare at the guy's head in front of
> you the whole flight. **Be a Man**

Over the last couple of hundred years, we've seen technology explode. We have seen the invention of the telephone, camera, electric lights, radio, airplanes, TV, and computers. Each of these newly created industries then created jobs and opportunities for millions of people to thrive. Although these electronic devices make it easier for us to communicate and travel and look at boobs, they also make it easier for us to work ourselves to death or get fat or get yelled at for looking at boobs. So maybe take the time to appreciate the simple things in life.

> Don't send emails. Write a letter by hand
> and deliver it in person. **Be a Man.**

These days, we are lucky. If we want a steak or some peanut butter, we just go to the store and pick something out off the shelf. During the Stone Age, the caveman's day would revolve around hunting and gathering for their next meal. Sometimes, it might take a whole day's work just to get enough for the family to eat one meal. There were no marinades, dressing, and sauces. Food was bland and simple. No chipotle mayo, no lemon pepper, no Old Bay Seasoning. These days, we have luxuries that we take for granted like soap to clean our hands and towels to dry them. It doesn't mean we have to use them.

> Never use a napkin. Just wipe the grease
> all over your pants. **Be a Man.**

We don't take kindly to doctors and medical procedures. We like to cut splinters out of our hands with utility knives and we cut our own hair with clippers. We never like to burden other people; we are truly self-sufficient beings. When we do get something fixed or altered, we keep it to ourselves and take it to the grave. Neanderthals weren't the greatest communicators and we haven't evolved very much since.

> If you have a tumor, rip it out with
> your bare hands. **Be a Man.**

Safety Last

Since we were young in shop class or working with our dads in the yard, we were taught to practice safety first. Most times, we throw caution to the wind in the hopes of getting the job done faster. It's not until some permanent damage happens that we ever learn our lesson.

> Bungee jump in a parking lot. **Be a Man.**

When something bad does happen, I was always taught to get right back on the horse. If an accident occurs and we're afraid to get back in the saddle, anxiety will quickly become a worse problem than the injury itself. And our anxiety only grows over time, so the longer we stay away, the worse it gets. The best solution is just to face it head on. Maybe wearing eye protection this time though.

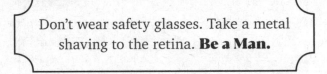

Don't wear safety glasses. Take a metal shaving to the retina. **Be a Man.**

I'm not sure, do we love pain or do we just hate other people telling us what is best for us? When I was a kid playing baseball, they always stressed the importance of a jockstrap and a protective cup. But when I wore my jockstrap and cup, it reduced the little mobility I had in the first place and hurt my balls when I ran. Of course, they stuck me at third base, where bullets from right-handed batters were launched at you every third hitter. What doesn't kill us, makes us stronger. Or maybe it just makes us shoot blanks.

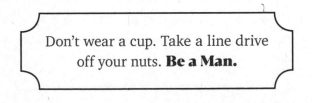

Don't wear a cup. Take a line drive off your nuts. **Be a Man.**

I'm a beach guy but I've never been a huge swimming guy. Instead of hopping on a surfboard or swimming out to the breakers, I'd much rather sit on a chair with a cooler and check out the broads.

> Never show your feet in public. **Be a Man.**

There would always be warnings about how there was a nasty riptide or there were sharks in the water. All of these warnings usually went in one ear and out the other. One day, it was hot as hell on the beach. I'd been drinking all day so I thought I'd hop in the water to cool off. Next thing you know, the riptide pulled me out and a quick dip turned into a forty-five-minute battle for my life. I swam and swam trying to get back to shore but it seemed like I was going nowhere. The harder I kicked and pulled, the more tired I got. I started to question if I had enough in the tank to actually make it back. I decided I would try to relax my body and sink under the water for a minute to catch my breath before giving it one final last push. If this didn't do it, I would just have to yield my body to the icy depths and a watery grave. I took a deep breath and ducked my head under the water. As my body dropped down, my feet immediately hit the sand. I was only up to my neck. I walked the rest of the way in.

> If you get stung by a jellyfish, piss on your leg. **Be a Man.**

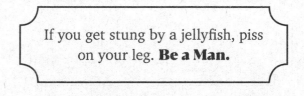

We're supposed to take all safety shit seriously, but of all the safety issues we don't take seriously, fire is the worst. If a candle tips over or a cigarette falls on the couch and sets it ablaze, trying to stop an inferno or even getting out unscathed is almost impossible.

When the fire alarms went off at school, they would teach us how to exit the building calmly and safely. If we were in the house during a fire, they taught us how to scale down the wall after climbing out of your bedroom window. If we actually caught on fire, they taught us how to stop, drop, and roll to put the fire out. When I was a kid, I was pumped for my house to catch fire; man, I was ready.

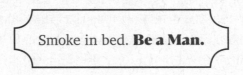

Smoke in bed. **Be a Man.**

Of course, in hindsight, this fire safety shit seems like a pipe dream. They say two-thirds of all fire-related deaths are caused by smoke inhalation after smoke detectors don't go off, either faulty units or dead batteries.

If your smoke detector keeps beeping, don't change the batteries. Chuck it out the window. **Be a Man.**

FIVE HOME SAFETY TIPS

1. Keep an expired fire extinguisher around just for looks.

2. Use your bare hand to clear a jammed blender or garbage disposal.

3. Don't bother turning off the power to work on the wiring (that breaker doesn't work anyway).

4. If you break a glass, just pick up the big pieces by hand, don't sweep.

5. Lock the kids in their rooms every night, you don't want those little shits getting out.

On Your Own

The only way you really get to know yourself is to spend a long stretch of time alone. Sometimes this happens fresh out of high school, sometimes it's in your twenties when you're working on an oil rig or as a bookie, sometimes it's in your thirties when you go away for a couple of years for working as a bookie. It doesn't matter how you get there, just make sure to take advantage of this alone time in your work camp or solitary confinement or whatever. This is when we truly find ourselves. Worst-case scenario, you might not be alone for the first time until you get out of a bad marriage in your forties. Even then, you're not unsalvageable. But you have a lot of catching up to do. Rot in your own filth. This is who you are.

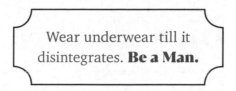

Wear underwear till it disintegrates. **Be a Man.**

We try not to exert any extra effort or put time into meaningless things when we are alone. We keep minimal plates and utensils on hand so we never have to clean more than one thing. One pan, one plate, and one fork are ideal. It's not like we host dinner parties. Maybe two plates so one can be an ashtray. We never truly sit down to eat, we would rather do it standing at the counter or shouting at the TV or driving in the car.

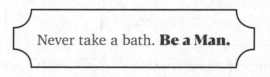

Don't use a plate. Eat over the sink. **Be a Man.**

When men are in relationships, we love to spend time in the bathroom to enjoy our quiet solitude. Living alone, we seem to get in and out of the shitter and the shower in a matter of minutes. While women can soak in Epsom salts for hours, you will only find us lying down in a bathroom when we are passed out on the floor.

Never take a bath. **Be a Man.**

When it comes to decorating, there isn't much we do in this department. We don't believe in tablecloths, framed pictures on walls, a million lamps in every room, area rugs, throw pillows, throw blankets, or curtains. A home is a cave to us. We just need a place to sleep, eat, and shit.

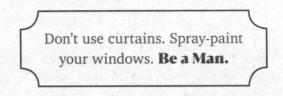

Don't use curtains. Spray-paint your windows. **Be a Man.**

We don't stock up on canned foods and stack them in the pantry or buy a ton of meat and put it in the deep freezer. We don't make big fancy meals on Sunday and prep them for the rest of the week. Most times, we eat the same shit every day. When we find something easy to cook that we like, we stick to it. Why bother washing the pan when you're just gonna use it to warm up Gorton's Fish Sticks again tomorrow? But inevitably, there will come a time when food in the house is low, and we are too lazy to do anything about it.

Don't go food shopping. Starve . . . die. **Be a Man.**

When you live with people and you lose something, you always have someone to blame. But when it's just you on your own and the remote control goes missing, there is no scapegoat. If you look hard for ten minutes and it is nowhere to be found, don't obsess about it. Just hop on your phone and take care of business.

Lose something? Don't look for it. Buy a new one. **Be a Man.**

FIVE KEYS TO LIVING ALONE

1. **CREATE A ROUTINE.** Wake up late for work in your clothes on the couch, brush your teeth in the truck on the way to work, work till your eyes are crossing, come home, turn on the TV, open a beer, wake up late for work in your clothes on the couch.

2. **GET SOME HOBBIES.** Like collecting ammunition and dead cars, taxidermy, and baseball cards.

3. **LEARN HOW TO COOK THE BASICS.** Every man should have some basic cooking skills. Buy a George Foreman grill and make every meal on it—chicken, steak, eggs, sandwiches, and quesadillas. Bon appetite.

4. **GET A DOG.** He'll be helpful cleaning up around the place, eating your leftover Taco Bell, and drinking any spilled beer. Kick a window out for a dog door.

5. **ENJOY YOUR FREEDOM.** This is what you wanted, right?

Law and Order

Law and order are of central importance to men because they're
some of the few things that stand in the way of us acting like complete assholes. This code of right and wrong pushes us to stay on the
right path. Don't get me wrong, I'm not saying we follow the laws.
Everybody speeds, no one wears their seat belts, and you're a complete knucklehead if you pull permits for every renovation project
and pay all of your taxes. There are some laws set in stone: don't kill
anybody if you can help it, don't kick a guy when he's down, don't
steal another guy's dog unless the dog would be a lot happier with

you, tip your bartender. But the laws that are the most important to us are the ones we create for ourselves.

> Don't get a lawyer. Do the whole bid. **Be a Man.**

All men seem to create a personalized rulebook that is filled with wild and random laws. We abide by these laws to a tee for no apparent reason. Sometimes we are very conscious we are doing it and other times we do it out of pure habit. And when our private rulebook runs up against someone else's, look out. I had a friend once tell me that his wife wanted me to remove my shoes or I had to leave. I haven't talked to him since. Sometimes these laws are so important to us that we are willing to risk everything.

> If you're going to someone's house, never take off your shoes. **Be a Man.**

When I was a kid, all we did was play sports. We would be out day and night, practicing slap shots and tossing around the football. My dad was over the top when it came to superstition. At an early age, he taught me that the only way to throw and shoot was right-handed. He thought that being a lefty was a curse and a bad omen. So even though shooting lefty always felt more natural for me, even though I could throw the ball fifteen yards farther as a lefty, I had to lock that up and throw away the key. This was the first time I learned how to turn my weaknesses into my strengths.

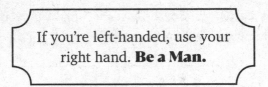

If you're left-handed, use your right hand. **Be a Man.**

Men are far from perfect. Sometimes we enjoy taking the easy route even if we don't realize we are. We drop ice cubes on the floor and kick them under the fridge. When we use up the last of the ice cubes, we put the empty trays back in the freezer. And then we yell the next time we go to the freezer and there's no ice. We won't eat onion dip if someone has double dipped the same chip but we insist on wearing our dirty shoes into the house and if we drop something on the floor, it's still OK to eat it off the floor if we grab it in less than five seconds, which ends up being more like thirty. So some of our rules come from our self-imposed morals, others are unknowingly ingrained in us from the previous generation, and others are just complete bullshit that come from who knows where.

Stand by the microwave for the whole cycle so you can stop it with one second left so you don't have to listen to the beep. **Be a Man.**

The Male Decline: Soft Boys

Over the past couple of decades, men have gotten softer and softer and softer. I grew up in a time when you needed to know how to change your own oil, fix a flat tire, tie a tie, and build a campfire. When we used to watch TV as kids, we saw men playing cowboys, soldiers, and superheroes—role models we looked up to. These characters taught us to be brave and strong and resourceful and to never, ever wear your heart on your sleeve.

> Never let someone know how much they mean to you until it's too late. **Be a Man**

A lot has changed over the years. For a while, women were real critical of men. We were expected to go to art openings, manscape, and use napkins. But isn't it interesting that nowadays it seems that some of the voices that are the loudest are women looking for the elusive "real men"? These women are attracted to big, strong animals who can build them houses and fix their cars and take care of any situation that might arise on the street. All that are left these days are man-sized boys in flannel shirts with hipster beards who drink craft beers and talk about video games all day. It's good to read a book now and then but it's become normalized for men to be so sensitive and self-centered that they are weak and helpless.

> Don't use a welding mask. Fuck up your eyes. **Be a Man.**

When I was young, we would move out of our parents' house as soon as humanly possible. Having our own freedom—not having to play by someone else's rules or having a list of chores and responsibilities hanging over our heads—that was something we dreamed about from the minute we were out of diapers. These days, guys live in their parents' basement into their thirties, afraid to leave the nest and try to survive on their own. They use their parents' credit cards to buy useless plastic crap on Amazon and go to the bar. As long as you fight to stay somebody else's child, you will never be a man. These guys run from the car to the house because they are afraid of raccoons in the trash barrels and they won't go downstairs at night without a Pokémon flashlight because they are afraid of the dark.

> Don't turn on the lights. Trip and break your neck. **Be a Man.**

I never even heard about food allergies until I was in my forties. As a kid, if you ate something that didn't agree with you, you were sent upstairs to sleep it off. If you said your stomach hurt every time you ate bread, your father would say, "Stop being a baby." If you puked every time you ate shellfish, it wasn't because you were allergic, it was because you were selfish and ungrateful and didn't appreciate good food.

> Have a nut allergy? Eat a peanut butter and jelly sandwich, see if God really wants you here. **Be a Man.**

The worst sin of all in this new world of men who are soft as baby food is fishing for compliments and validation. *Oh, you made the bed you slept in? You took out the trash you made? Did you pack your own lunch for school too?* These men feel entitled to praise they know they don't deserve, something they will never deserve. Anytime someone thinks they deserve a gold star just because they did a little bit of work, they don't deserve it. The people who deserve it are the ones that aren't showing off and fishing for any accolades, the people who do work just to do work. The only reward in this life is getting the job done, and the job is only done when you're dead.

> Compliments are for broads, never accept them. **Be a Man.**

The Great Communicator

Men and women are just built differently. We're built differently and we magnify those differences in our minds. Most men think that women talk way too much. We actually talk just as much as they do. The main difference is that we talk about tools, sports, and cars, while broads spend most of their time focused on relationships. The only relationship we're interested in is the one between Brady and Belichick, or maybe the beef between the heavyweights for the fight on Saturday night. Most other men couldn't care less about what relationship we're involved in. We're not here to talk about feelings and emotions and if we did, we sure as hell wouldn't talk to the boys about it.

> Don't want to answer a question?
> Mumble the answer. **Be a Man.**

Men and women approach major life issues and the little things that happen on a daily basis in completely different ways. We ignore the big questions so we can devote ourselves to details that don't really matter in the grand scheme of things. We never think about mortality or true love or the meaning of life so we can give our full attention to shit like hockey stats, alcohol content, horsepower, and portion sizes. Of course, the little details women want us to pay attention to, yeah, those we ignore. When our girl asks us to go out to the store to grab a few things, we hop in the car and hear a good song and turn up the radio and then drive around for a few hours, then come home empty-handed.

> Never make a shopping list. Just forget half of the shit you were supposed to get. **Be a Man.**

By nature, men are not the most social beings. We don't go out and mingle unless it is assisted by alcohol. When we get stuck in conversations we don't want to be in, we find excuses to get out by saying things like, "I gotta take a piss," or "Let me take this call." The best party I can think of would be sitting home alone on the couch with a drink, watching the highlights of the Patriots' 28–3 Super Bowl comeback for the millionth time. When we do have to go to a big party of a hundred people or more, we spend the least amount of time we have to be there, then disappear into the night.

> Never say good-bye to anyone.
> Just leave. **Be a Man.**

When we go somewhere with our girl, they always want us to be hanging out with them the whole night. When I go out to get a few drinks, I don't want to sit in the corner, talking to the same person I talk to every single night. I want to see what this place has to offer. If it's a family event, I wanna check out the food display, see what kind of drinks are in the cooler, and catch up with the cousins. I don't like to be held down when I'm out. I like to roam free. Congrats, you got me off the couch and out of the house, take the win and go talk to someone else about it.

Take your girl to a family party and then don't talk to her all day. **Be a Man.**

Respect

Respect is a code we were taught to live by when I was young. If we didn't respect the people older than us, we got our asses whooped. Everyone is raised differently under different circumstances but respect should be at the core of what any kid is taught. Learning about respect—how to show it and how to get it—helped to shape who I've become. We all knew we wanted to be treated with respect but it took a while to figure out that it started with respecting ourselves and the people around us.

> Treat the janitor with the same respect as the CEO. **Be a Man.**

Too often, we take people for granted and feel entitled—entitled to sit where we want, entitled to be treated a certain way, entitled to own a certain phone or drive a certain car. No matter who you are or where you come from, always remember that in this lifetime, no one owes you jack shit. Any time someone does something good for you, make sure to return the favor, and with interest.

> Help someone before they ask for it. **Be a Man.**

There will be times when we lose our cool. When tempers flare, our behavior may get out of line and we compromise our core values but that's all part of learning who we are. We can never take that out on people because of who they are or how they live. You drag one of those people down, you better be back there the next day, building them up.

> Act like nobody's better than you and there's nobody worse than you. **Be a Man.**

My dad raised me to be independent, to stand on my own two feet. I tried my best to do the same with my kids. The best, most important lessons I got growing up didn't happen in the classrooms but on the ball fields, at the gas station, in the grocery store, and in the streets. When you show a healthy level of respect for yourself and the people around you, it changes your work, your ethics, and your entire approach to life.

The Rock of the Family

As much as my father taught me how to be a man, it was my mother who built our confidence and kept us grounded. My dad led by example so he was always out working. My mother was the one who raised us and really instilled our core values.

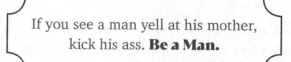

If you see a man yell at his mother, kick his ass. **Be a Man.**

She constantly had us doing chores to earn our keep. We had to vacuum the floors, clean the yard, do the laundry, and pick the vegetables. My mother is the kindest person I've ever known and she showed a lot of patience. But when we got out of line and started being little pricks, out came the yardstick. She would turn into "The General" to restore order.

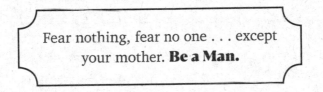

Fear nothing, fear no one . . . except your mother. **Be a Man.**

I was more fortunate than most. Growing up, I had one of the best moms in the world. She always bent over backward in order to support us and teach us the right way to do shit. From a very young age, she did everything she could to make sure we understood the world. And she made a special point to make sure we appreciated the value of a dollar. She grew up poor, in a one-room apartment, so she taught us never to take shit for granted and to feel grateful for everything we had.

Bust your ass your whole life to make enough money to buy toys for your spoiled kids that they never use. **Be a Man.**

I know a lot of people weren't as lucky growing up as I was. If you have a bad relationship with your mom, it can really mess you up mentally for years. Any time I started to stray in the wrong direction, I heard the words my mother had ingrained in my head. So in a lot of ways, that kept me on the right track.

> Ignore your mother's advice your whole life till you have kids, then yell the same shit at them. **Be a Man.**

Mothers are the greatest when it comes to multitasking and being resourceful. My mom was a legend in our eyes. Any time we needed something, she delivered because that's what good moms do. She taught sewing and worked as a seamstress. We didn't have a ton of money when we were growing up so she made all of our clothes. They looked better than anything you saw in a department store and they lasted way longer.

> Treat your mother like crap when you're a kid, then spend the rest of your life trying to make up for it. **Be a Man.**

After being a homemaker for many years, my mother had to go out and find a good-paying job to provide for us when my parents divorced. This is when we really saw our mom rise above it once again. With her back against the wall, she went out and became a mortgage broker with no formal training. In the next twenty years, she became one of the most successful brokers around Boston, winning all sorts of awards. My mother never went to college but the experiences she had over the years were far more helpful than any formal education.

> It's OK if your wife doesn't get along with your mother because you can get a new wife. **Be a Man.**

It's only natural for a kid to grow up and not see eye to eye with their parents from time to time but the key is to never stray too far away. Don't burn that bridge. No matter how much your mother drives you nuts or nags the shit out of you, it's the strong bond with our mothers that gives us the strength to move mountains.

> Talk shit about your mom. If someone else joins in, knock their teeth in. **Be a Man.**

Shitting the Bed

When we're young, we can read a sign on the highway from a mile away, hear a conversation two rooms over, and run five miles without breaking a sweat. People always warn us that the shit we do when we're young will catch up to us one day, but we just double down and go harder.

> Turn the volume all the way up and blow out your eardrums. **Be a Man.**

For the first twenty years of my life, I truly believed that no matter how hard I got hit or got hurt, if I got to my feet quickly, I was gonna be fine. It's not actually true, but I believed it hard enough that it was for me. For twenty years, anyway. Pain comes in all shapes and sizes. It can be the black hole in your chest you get when someone close to you dies, an agonizing sharp pain when you fall on ice, or a burning sensation when you piss. Pain, in all its forms, is inevitable. But the real question is how you handle it.

> If you fall down the stairs, don't make a sound. **Be a Man.**

Anytime I got out of a pickup truck as a teenager, I jumped from the bed onto the pavement and the vibration ran from my heels all the way up my spine. When I played baseball, I'd play catcher in a doubleheader with my legs folded in awkward positions for four hours while getting a case of heat stroke in the process.

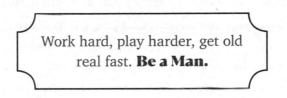

Work hard, play harder, get old real fast. **Be a Man.**

Soon enough, these shocks to our bodies start to cause major deterioration. Before we know it, we can barely walk or hear people talk or make out who the actor is on the TV. It would be easy to just bitch and complain about it, but it is something we did to ourselves by ignoring repeated warnings. There's really only one thing you can do when your own idiotic decisions have put you in a bad situation: find a way to use it to your advantage.

If you can't hear someone, just nod your head and say, "Sounds good." **Be a Man.**

The last, or at least the most important thing, to shit the bed is our dick. Maybe we didn't do anything intentional to mess this one up but the fact that we've been eating like shit and not exercising enough hasn't helped matters. This is the one loss that hurts the most. If your hearing is gone and you can't make out what your mother-in-law is saying, that's not a big deal. If your back hurts and you can't do your coworker's dumb "walk for hunger," you'll live. But when you want a little blood flow to still feel alive and it just won't work, that is truly a sad day.

> If your dick doesn't work, yell at it. **Be a Man.**

End of the Road

There are about a million reasons why men live shorter lives than women. First and foremost, it's always the larger animals in nature that die first. We work too hard for too long, and we carry more weight and stress, which contributes to a ton of underlying health problems over time. But that is just the tip of the iceberg. We work more dangerous jobs like construction, coal mining, ocean fishing, and roofing. When we drink, we drink double. When we smoke, we smoke triple. We are reckless and we do everything to the extreme. When it comes to going to the doctor and taking care of our health, we avoid it like the plague. We get a physical once every decade and when we get a finger caught in the table saw, we tape it back on till it heals.

> Don't ask for help until it's too late. **Be a Man.**

When girls are growing up, they're taught to have fun by playing with dolls and playing dress-up. The forms of entertainment for boys are animalistic and dangerous. We tackle each other, wrestle in the yard, and box in the driveway. We have rock fights. For us, fun and entertainment is measured by how hard you get hit, how many stars you see, and how many stitches it took till it stopped bleeding. It's no wonder that women are the last ones standing.

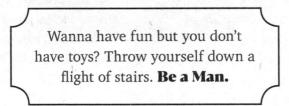

> Wanna have fun but you don't have toys? Throw yourself down a flight of stairs. **Be a Man.**

Men don't fear death, we embrace it. We know that when you don't take care of yourself, you ignore vitamins and nutrition and exercise, you refuse any kind of medication or medical care your entire life, there will come a point when your luck will run out. Men have come to grips with that. We're not lying awake in bed, afraid we're going to die. We're afraid we're going to live too long. And the only way we truly feel alive is when we dive into the middle of the storm and stare fear directly in the face. High blood pressure? Heart disease? Cancer? Men feel no sense of urgency. I'm not gonna go out of my way to do something I don't want to do. We learned to live with the consequences of our decisions a long time ago. We're ready to die with them too.

> High cholesterol? Eat a double bacon cheeseburger and large fries. **Be a Man.**

I've always believed that when it's your time, it's your time. When I go, I don't want everyone to be sad or depressed. I want there to be a full-fledged party where people can go up to the microphone and give the crowd their best "Be a Man," an out-of-control, eight-keg rager where they shut down the whole block until finally someone calls the cops at four in the morning because the party just won't stop. Leaving a legacy is important to a man, whether that is through your kids, your ideals, or your accomplishments. As long as the Mafia continues to spread the word that it's OK to be manly, then I've done my job. Just make sure they bury me in my *Be a Man* shirt with my white hat on backward.

> When the fire alarm goes off, grab a six-pack and sit on the couch. **Be a Man.**

The Be a Man Mafia

The last couple of years have been an absolute whirlwind as the Be a Man movement has grown from one tiny little idea and then spread all around the world. In a time when people are more sensitive than ever, our job has been to show the world that it's OK to still be manly. We've been lucky enough to carve our niche into a world gone mad. We know we can be difficult but we are also hardworking, passionate, and resourceful and there is nothing wrong with that.

The Be a Man Mafia has grown to include people of all walks of life from around the globe. We have banded together as a family behind one simple concept: it's still OK to be a man. This family isn't just for men, either. Women have found comfort in the movement as well. For the first time in a ten-year relationship or a twenty-year marriage, these wives and girlfriends are starting to understand that they are not alone. The ridiculous, stubborn animal you married isn't a unique specimen or an isolated case. He's part of a tribe, a tribe formed more than a hundred thousand years ago that killed what they ate and stared for endless hours each night at a fire they made by rubbing two sticks together. We are simple beings and the faster everyone can understand that, the better off we will all be. Don't try to change us, appreciate us for what we are . . . MEN!

THE TEN BE-A-MANDMENTS

1. Sundays are for grilling and football.

2. Never hit on your neighbor's wife, but it's OK to hit on her sister.

3. Never be seen with cops unless you're getting arrested.

4. Always be five minutes early.

5. Thou shall not kill, unless it is your dinner or they mess with your friends and family.

6. Always treat women with respect.

7. Never be jealous, but always be suspicious.

8. Never snitch, always mumble the answer.

9. Do the right thing.

10. Always be available for the Be a Man Mafia. You are always on call—even if your wife's giving birth.

Contradict yourself daily. **Be a Man.**

ACKNOWLEDGMENTS

This goes out to all the men across the world who have never changed for anyone. To all the good dads and even to all the shitty ones who didn't know any better. To all the blue-collar warriors who bang nails, hang sheetrock, install toilets, cut grass, shingle roofs, lay asphalt, or cut hair for a living. To all the men who have served in the military. To all the hustlers who are never satisfied with the status quo and always push to be great and want more. To anyone who works a thankless job but still gets up every day and does their job the right way.

To Uncle Libby and Uncle Nacco, who taught me about respect and making money. To my dad, Eugene, who kept me in line and showed me that hard work and loyalty were everything.

To everyone over at UTA but most importantly to Byrd Leavell and Dan Milaschewski: you guys helped us navigate an unfamiliar world and made it as simple and easy as possible. Byrd, you are a badass who plays by your own rules and we are happy to have you on our side. Dan, you have been great every step of the way, you're just getting started and we can't wait to see all the great things you do.

To our people over at HarperCollins, thanks for believing in *Be a Man*, especially Doug Jones, who reached out early on and saw the potential of what this could be—we will never forget that. To Noah Eaker, your professionalism and contributions have helped to keep our vision intact and in line with the brand.

To Mishka Shubaly, who was brought on to help take a bunch of crazy ideas and make it all make sense; we couldn't have got it here without you. Thanks for your dedication, creativity, and advice. If we ever do anything like this again, we won't do it without you.

To the Breaking Balls crew who have been grinding for years to make this work even when no one else believed. Your vision has turned Be a Man into a global movement that appeals to people from all walks of life in ways we never could have imagined. Joe, Tonzo and Mr. Monday: thanks for being relentless and never giving up.

To my partner in crime, John Fiore, on the *Be a Man Experience* podcast. Your humor, knowledge, and creativity have been integral to the success of the project. Salute.

To everyone that I forgot, go fuck yourselves.

> Forget everything, forget everyone. **Be a Man.**

ABOUT THE AUTHOR

THE BE A MAN GUY was born in the late 1950s in East Boston, Massachusetts. He spent the majority of his early years working at his family's bar, the American House Café, which forced him to learn the business and grow up faster than the other kids in the neighborhood. By the age of eight, he started hustling and learning how to run the books for his uncles, collecting money and taking bets. This early action taught him what it meant to be stoic, stubborn, and work hard. These years helped to form the foundation for *Be a Man*.

After years of doing every type of work and hustle there is, the Be a Man guy compiled so much manly wisdom that people would come from miles around to hear it. By 2020, people were pestering him for advice so much that he started a TikTok account in order to get them off his back. Boy, did that backfire. Within a couple of months @bostonbeaman had become an internet phenomenon as fans started sharing the videos and sending in their versions of Be a Mans by the hundreds every day. Today, more than six million people follow the accounts across TikTok, Instagram, and YouTube to get their daily dose of manly advice.